Car$

The Ins and Outs of Buying and Selling

Brooks R Fiesinger

Car$- The Ins and Outs of Buying and Selling

Current contact information is available at
BrooksFiesinger.com

ISBN: 1495257029
ISBN-13: 978-149525702

Table of Contents:

ACKNOWLEDGMENTS

I have great appreciation for all the dealers, experts, and companies who offered additional insights into their shops and efforts during the writing of this book. I would like to thank W. Jean Fiesinger and Jessica L Fiesinger for their editing and writing insights. Additionally, I would like to thank Paranoid Production Designs Inc. and Active Word Fonts for allowing me to use their proprietary, patented typography tools for versions of this book (Patent 8,239,763), and for their ClassicRead font for all others.

Most Importantly, I want to thank you, the reader, for taking the time to improve your vehicular buying and selling, and for choosing this book as one source for your insights.

Car$- The Ins and Outs of Buying and Selling

About the Author

Brooks Fiesinger has been an owner and executive of five different automotive-industry businesses, in addition to his Adjunct Professorship. He has presented Marketing to Generation Y at the North American International Auto Show, better known as the Detroit Auto Show. He has won awards and recognitions in Innovation and patented new inventions, as well as developed new processes and products for the automotive industry.

Brooks Fiesinger, received his MBA from Syracuse University's Whitman School of Management, and currently teaches Marketing & Entrepreneurship courses. In addition, he is an Entrepreneur who successfully purchases and resells 4-7 cars per year. Starting as a hobby 15 years ago, he has gained a reputation for rarely losing money, even on new car purchases, and has successfully purchased and resold cars without losses in all areas of the market, from sports cars to luxury cars, collector cars to commuter cars, trucks to convertibles, new cars to used cars, and even motorcycles, snowmobiles, trailers, and ATVs. This has lead to continued requests for advice and assistance in car sales and car purchases which led to the creation of this guide.

Fiesinger has compiled this resource by simplifying the more complex marketing and entrepreneurship basics commonly accepted in academia and businesses, by applying them to the process of buying, maintaining, and selling cars for the typical owner. He challenges the common notions that car purchases must be an expensive "cost" and instead offers methods to maintain quality automotive ownership without the traditional burdens of the expenses. His tips for automotive buying can help everyone make the most informed car purchases, and he offers advanced methods for people hoping to buy and sell cars without losing money, and even make money in automotive ownership.

Coupling his experience, research, and business expertise with interviews and input from new and used car salesmen, dealership owners, and service mechanics, Fiesinger unlocked the mysteries of car buying and selling in a comprehensive, fact-based method.

Introduction

This guide is based on the concept of net-neutral and net-positive car ownership. In other words, buying cars without the long term "high cost" of cars by allowing buyers to purchase cars for the same price or less, than the prices at which they sell them. The term "Net" is a business term used frequently in finance, and ultimately means "total amount after all included costs and taxes have been paid." "Net Income" is a company's income minus expenses. "Net Profit" is referring to the total profitability of a company after all costs are accounted for. "Net sales" are the total sales revenue after removing losses and returns. In this case, "net-neutral" means that the total cost of acquiring the car, including any repair costs, tax costs, purchasing costs, or inspection costs remains the same as the amount it would be resold for, and "net-positive" means that the total cost of acquiring the car is lower than the amount it would be resold for.

Owning cars net-neutral and net-positive takes

additional research and at times additional efforts as a buyer and as a seller. While almost anyone can achieve net-neutral and net-positive car ownership, many individuals will choose to "pay" for convenience. Even for those who aren't seeking net-neutral and net-positive car ownership, this guide will offer insight and financial business-based perspectives to assure the buyer maximizes his or her financial position throughout any part of the car ownership process.

Section 1:

Buying a Car

Buying a Car

The basics of acquiring a good deal on both a new or used car are the same. It follows the basic economic principle of supply and demand. If a car is a high profile, in-demand car, then demand is high and supply is low, therefore the price will be at a premium. On the other hand, a car that is not in demand will offer low prices as the demand is low and the supply is high. This drives prices down.

For those not familiar with the concept of supply and demand, it is fairly straight forward. Buyers and sellers strive to match up to meet each other's need for a sale. If there are 5 buyers and 5 sellers for example, each buyer will match with a seller and everyone selling will successfully sell, and every buyer will successfully buy, leaving everyone satisfied. When there are more people selling something than buying, then the sellers have to compete for the buyer. In this case there may be 8 sellers and 5 buyers. In this case, the 5 buyers will still only buy from 5 sellers, but they will pick the ones that meet their needs best, leaving 3 sellers without a buyer, and unable to satisfy their need to sell. Since each seller does not want to be left without a buyer, through competition they will each work to make a buyer choose what they are selling. This may be through advertisements, conditions and features, or often price. Only the 5 sellers who accept the lowest prices will sell, and the remaining 3 are left without a buyer. When there are more sellers than buyers, the price typically is pushed downwards. This is what is meant by the phrase "High Supply, Low Demand". On the other hand, if there were 7 buyers and only 5 sellers, then only 5 buyers can be satisfied, and 2 buyers will be unable to match up with a seller. The sellers will sell to the buyers who will pay the most, driving the prices up.This means that the buyers will instead compete for the sellers. Only the 5 buyers who will pay the most will buy, and the remaining two will be left without a car to purchase. When there are more buyers than sellers, the price is pushed upwards. This is what is meant by the phrase "Low Supply, High Demand". Buyers get the best deal when there is high supply and low demand. Sellers on the other hand get the best deal when there is low supply and high demand.

While the basics of supply and demand is the most significant driver of car prices, the actual deal opportunities cannot be confined to this relatively simple concept. There are other factors that influence the ultimate purchase price, and these include holding costs for the dealerships (Inventory taxes and floor plan lending), quota's, sales cycles, tax incentives, used car demand, as well as other unique factors.

A second specific factor of purchasing prices is leverage. When discussing the buying and selling of cars, leverage is the additional advantage given to a buyer or seller due to the specific circumstances of each party. For example, when a buyer recently wrecked his or her last car, a seller knows he or she must purchase a replacement car right away. This gives the seller additional leverage because they know there is a cost to not getting the deal completed quickly, as the potential buyer must go through the day to day hassles of not having a car. Therefore a seller will know it is in a buyers best interest to pay a premium to purchase a car quickly. On the other hand, a buyer looking for a spare car to enjoy when the weather is nice will decrease a sellers leverage because there is no cost to continually looking at other cars and spending time searching and negotiating. A buyer can gain leverage when a seller needs to sell a car quickly, such as when they are moving abroad or they purchased another car and can't afford two payments, or a dealer has to hit quotas or wants to prevent added holding costs. In these situations, a buyer can gain significant leverage. Whether buying or selling, finding ways to assure that leverage is achieved will often lead to making more money as a seller or saving more money as a buyer. It is also imperative not to alert the other party if the other party does have leverage. For example, if a buyer needs a car quickly, it may not be in their best interest to tell the seller this, as letting the seller know they have leverage will often lead them to act on it.

A great example of this situation is when the author purchased a BMW. The seller let the author know that he was planning on trading the car in the next day on the purchase of another car. The author was then able to analyze what the trade-in price would be and make an offer just slightly above it, yet well below current market value. Since the author knew he had leverage, he knew he could acquire the vehicle with a low offer. The buyer accepted the offer since it was still higher than what he would have gotten as a trade in- However, if the seller had not alerted the buyer that the car was likely to be traded (or was able to hold off trading the car in), the author likely would have offered a higher amount, allowing the seller to make more money from the sale.

A second way to help maintain positive leverage as a buyer or seller is to assure all necessary research has been completed, so one is prepared to quickly act when the opportunity arises. As both a buyer and a seller, often great deals are available with very short notice when an opposing seller or buyer's leverage is low. By not being in a rush as a buyer, a leverage difference is not lost in the favor of the seller, helping to prevent the buyer from being in a situation where they are overpaying due to leverage. A buyer is often left with poor leverage when their old car breaks down or when they are overly eager to buy when their tax refund arrives. As a seller on the other hand, not being rushed to sell a car will prevent them from having a leverage difference in the buyer's favor, preventing a seller from being forced to sell under value. These scenarios where a seller loses leverage to a buyer include situations when a major bill is due, or when a seller is about to trade in a car. By being prepared to sell, a seller can take advantage of a buyer whose leverage is low, allowing them to command top dollar. A prepared buyer can also take advantage of sellers whose leverage is low allowing them to command bottom dollar. The basics are straightforward- buyers and sellers alike should always seek ways to increase their leverage in relation to whomever they are negotiation.

After all of the "big picture" perspectives are considered, then the fine tuning of getting an improved deal comes down to specific negotiation and buying tactics which differ between new and used cars.

Choosing a Car

There is one rule of thumb that can be very difficult for many buyers: The pickier a buyer is with what they want, the more money they are going to pay for it. When a buyer is flexible with the cars they will take, they open themselves up for many more opportunities- including the opportunity to acquire a better car for a great price. The more specific a buyer is with what they demand, the less likely they will be to get a great deal.

There are many reasons why this is true. First and foremost is that once a buyer finds the car they really want, they become emotionally invested in the car. When emotionally invested in a car, buyers simply will pay more for the car because they are worried about the possibility of losing the opportunity to purchase it. As a buyer, in addition to simply seeking out the right types of cars, buyers often have to put offers on several cars before he or she gets the right car at the right price. Once becoming emotionally attached to a car, a buyer will negotiate a price with the seller, but loses one of their greatest leverage points, the ability to walk away and buy something else!

The second major issue with being specific in a car choice is that it limits the ability of a buyer to find the great deals when they are available. At any given time there are a large number of great deals on a variety of cars, but the more specific a buyer is, the less chance they'll find a great deal in that specific focus of car purchasing. Often buyers state things such as "I want a 2006-2009 Honda CRV in Red with an automatic transmission and heated leather seats with navigation". Upon searching for available cars with this set up, they will likely find only a few matching their purchase requirements, and the buyer will create their perceived value based on those available cars. This often means they may end up paying $5000 more for one car over another available car just because of the paint color, or even worse because of the seats when they would not consciously do so if they had realized how much price difference really existed between the alternatives.

Many vehicle options can be added to a car later, often for cheaper than a buyer would pay for it up front, especially when considering the "cost" of losing a car that is a great deal. As a buyer, the author rarely gets to pick up the exact option packages necessary, but he narrows down his requirements to the absolute bare minimums that are important for whatever purpose a car is being purchased for. High quality leather seats for a 4-door car can easily be added later for $600-1000. A high quality navigation system with Bluetooth and an improved sound system can be installed for $1000 or less. Other car options really are not a big deal once a buyer considers the actual extra cost they may be paying for it. An extra $4500 for a spoiler and some bigger wheels, or $6000 for chrome bumpers, wheels, and a specialized badge don't sound quite so appealing, even though the "book" value may only be a few hundred dollars for specific features, the prices are often driven up on some combinations while great deals are found in others. This difference can often be much higher than a buyer realizes when they are selecting their purchase focus.

One other major issue is that while a buyer certainly feels like an individual, he or she is often looking for the same packages and features as everyone else. This goes back to the basic principle of supply and demand. When there are a higher number of buyers, sellers command a higher price, driving up the cost. This may include paying $10,000 more for a hybrid version of a car than a non-hybrid, a cost difference that will never be made up in fuel savings no matter how long the car is owned, or specific colors, option packages, or unique features such as MP3 players, projector headlights, LED tail lights, and others that happen to be more popular today than they were when the car initially was sold.

This issue expands a little further than simply specific features and options. Often buyers want a specific popular car. It is important that a buyer expand their thought process to ask "why" they want that specific car, as price is relative to demand. In Economics this is called a "Supply and Demand Curve". As demand increases, and supply decreases, price increases. This works the other way as well. As supply increases and demand decreases, prices decrease. This is one of the reasons Corvettes almost always sell for well above book value, while a Geo sells for less.

To use this to a buyers benefit, often they must expand their search. They may be surprised to find out that at the time of this publishing, a buyer can pick up a 5 year old Jaguar X-Type with low mileage and good condition for $6200, while a similar condition 5 year old Honda Civic is $11,300. When investigating the Book Value, according to KBB.com, the Jaguar book value is around $13,000 while the

Civic is just over $11,000. A quick search at the major car listing locations shows this is not limited to specific finds, as the Jaguars are selling for well under book value- while Civics are selling at or above. This is precisely why it is important to expand the breadth of a car search. Many buyers may not realize that a car they'd prefer to have is actually cheaper, as they carry too many preconceived notions into the buying process. In this same scenario, the MSRP on the Jaguar was $35,000, and the Civic was only $18,710! For many, they may prefer this Jaguar over the Civic, but never would take the time to look due to their preconceived notions of pricing. To someone else on the other hand, they'd certainly prefer a Civic over the Jaguar. It is ultimately a personal decision, but a buyer with a $10,000 budget may have to step back to an older Civic, but would be perfectly happy with a newer Jaguar with money to spare.

The same preconceived notions that effect one buyer's behavior also impact the buying behavior and thought process of other buyers, which leads back to the concept of supply and demand. When a brand had a historically poor image, but began to produce better cars, the old preconceived brand image will still resonate with many buyers purchasing decisions, pulling down the used car value. The same thing also happens in reverse- A brand which historically has had a great reputation finds itself with major mechanical concerns regarding its recent generation of cars, and is not meeting expectations of it's brand. Still, even though the car fails to support it, buyers are often impacted by the historical brand value and positive brand image, influencing purchase behavior and in turn driving up purchase prices. It is for this reason that it can be dangerous to follow brands simply because of reputation. For example, when purchasing a new Ram 1500, the quality seemed to be great. There were a lot of great features, and customers that had them seemed to love them. The rebates, however, were so incredibly high, that a brand new one could be had for $14,000 under MSRP. Fast forward one more year and the same car wins several national awards, driving up demand, allowing the car to be sold used a year later for almost the same price it was new! It was the same identical car, but what changed was buyer opinions of the car, which drives prices up and down.

Choosing the right car often means buying slightly different. It is important for buyers to assure they do not follow "common beliefs" and "rules of thumb" on cars that hold value. For a car to be a good value, a buyer needs to maximize its value proposition against the market, not simply doing what everyone else does. In the stock market, if a buyer were to buy when everyone else is buying, and sell when everyone else is selling, they would constantly be losing money, selling low and buying high. The same logic applies to car purchasing.

When it comes down to the final offer and purchase decision, it is possible that the buyer sees something they like more for a little higher cost. There is nothing wrong with paying a little bit more for precisely what a buyer wants- However, all too often the buyer narrows down their requirements so early in the process, they fail to notice that the actual cost difference isn't "a little bit more"- but rather they are passing up a great deal, and are left paying much more for options that could easily be added later, or for features that really aren't that important.

When purchasing cars, especially new cars, many buyers turn to ratings and reviews agencies such as websites and magazines. While these resources are excellent and often offer significant beneficial information, it is important for buyers to take their findings with a grain of salt. Often these agencies will dock a car on items that don't bother specific buyers. "Hard plastic interior" on a Jeep may be a huge negative for a popular magazine, but to many Jeep owners, this is actually a positive, or at least not a negative. "Loud Road Noise" may be another negative, but during a test drove, a buyer may not even notice the road noise. Magazines often rate cars on things such as "design", but this is very intrinsic to the specific buyer. If a potential buyer likes the design, they should not let design ratings worry them, since a buyer can effectively evaluate those factors for themself. Instead, a buyer should focus on the ratings for topics which they cannot monitor themselves, such as safety ratings and reliability. Even in these areas however, it is important for buyers to educate themselves and determine what is behind the "stars". Some rating systems will actually dock points or ratings for factors which may not actually influence the factor being reviewed. In addition, a car may get a lower safety rating for something that is less concerning to you, such as rollover risk, while another car with the same rating had reduced points for something more concerning, such as safety in an accident. For these reasons it is important for buyers to look at the big picture, and not rush to judgment based on a limited set of factors.

Don't fall for the 24 hour test drive. Many dealers will attempt to get a buyer to try out the car for an entire day or two. Buyers, intending to be savvy, tell themselves they "won't fall for it." They insist they know it is not theirs and they won't fall into its grips. The salesperson knows better, however, and will push a buyer to it all the same. They do this because in spite of the buyer's knowledge and intention, it works. Even though a buyer tells themselves and their spouse that they will keep their distance, driving it into the buyer's comfort zone, parking it in their garage or at their apartment, grabbing some food or picking up groceries in it will make the prospective buyer fall in love with the car simply because of the newness of the experience, as the car assimilates into the buyer's daily life. The buyer's friends, family, and neighbors will oogle over the new car no matter what model it is. After all, any new car is interesting and exciting for a while. If a buyer takes the car for a 24 hour test drive, they have just as well already bought it. A salesperson, on the other hand, knows that since the buyer doesn't think they'll fall into the trap, a 24 hour test drive is a much easier sell than trying to get the buyer to complete the purchase that day. For this reason, savvy buyers skip the 24 hour test drives.

Regardless of the type of car of interest, from a sports car, to a van, to an SUV or sedan, when a buyer evaluates their needs from a larger perspective, and doesn't prematurely narrow down their purchase requirements, they open themselves up for more opportunities to secure great pricing, and get net-neutral or net-positive car ownership.

Don't Choose New or Used too Quickly!

Often buyers put themselves in "new" or "used" buying categories prematurely. While this may sound irrational, at times new cars can actually be cheaper than their used counterparts, especially when factoring in warranties, a trade in, rebates/discounts, and lower interest rates.

Some cars, such as pickup trucks and new model sports cars hold their value incredibly well. This can often mean that used cars may actually be priced above new cars! A buyer purchased a new model year 2011 Camaro LS in 2011. One year later, with several thousand miles on it, she was able to trade it in to a dealership for more than she had paid new! She chose to sell it for cash instead to move to complete debt-free vehicle ownership. She sold the car for just about $1500 less than the new purchase price to a dealer who marked it up and sold it off their lot. This actual car was sold a buyer who likely assumed they were out of new-car buying territory, and paid more for it used than the original buyer had paid for the same car brand new from the dealer floor! Another buyer was initially looking for a used truck, but was surprised how expensive low mileage, late model trucks cost. He found a brand new truck on the dealer floor right at the end of the dealer's fiscal year. He received so much off of MSRP that he ended up paying less than he would have for a used truck with similar options, noticeable mileage on it and a shorter warranty! In both scenarios, new car buying was actually a financially better deal than used car buying.

Although it depends on the state, new car buyers typically only pay sales tax on the difference between the trade and the new car. This is typically not true of used cars. This means that a wholesale-valued trade in purchased for $20,000 from a seller could be worth $2000 more to a seller's bottom line at a new car dealer than a used car dealer. This is $2000 that does not come from the dealer's pocketbook, so will not affect negotiations. Do note that this is dependent on the state. Consult a local dealership or accountant for specific information regarding your state's laws.

In addition, a new car purchase interest rates may see a 1.5% or more savings compared to that of a used car. This can be much more significant depending on the current interest rates. In one real-world example where a buyer was purchasing a $30,000 car with a $10,000 trade in, the difference in financing rates between a new and used car was $1,157.

Combining the interest rate difference and the sales tax benefit, a new car could actually offer $1500-3000 additional saved by a buyer than the actual final negotiated cost, making a "$37,000" used truck the same as a "$40,000" new truck. Case in point, a local Dodge dealer has a 2012 Ram 1500 Laramie listed for $38,988. Their bottom dollar is likely just over $37,000. It has 6,000 miles on it and 1 year left on its comprehensive warranty. On paper, this is a fair deal. Another dealership has a 2013 Ram Laramie with the same options (plus better gas mileage, better features, and higher resale on the 2013 model). This car including only publicly available rebates and discounts is offered for $38,000 bottom dollar from the dealership. The MSRP is $46,024. It includes the full 3 year warranty (5 year drivetrain), and has all identical features plus a few new features introduced in 2013. In this case, even though the bottom dollar is $1000 more, there would be a $2100 difference in financing costs if there were no trade in, plus as much as $2000 less paid in taxes with a $20,000 trade in. In both cases the new car is actually cheaper when considering the actual out of pocket cost, even if the list price and negotiated price is not lower.

New cars are sometimes discounted below used-car pricing. Depending on the option packages, local dealerships over the past two years have sold a number of brand new cars off the lots which were one to two model years old for $14,000-$16,000 under MSRP. While these situations are relatively rare, they do emerge and offer a tremendous opportunity to pick up a new car with full warranties, specific options, and full knowledge of its maintenance history for the same price or less- than a used car.

If new cars cost more than comparable used cars, sometimes the cost can be worth it. Full knowledge of the maintenance history, a full warranty, and the ability to get specific options a buyer wants are all reasons why new car ownership can be the best option. It is important to understand that a buyer typically has to "pay" for these advantages. This often means the car is worth less if they were to try to resell it than what they would pay new. If this is the case, it is important to have a significant enough trade in or down payment to assure the buyer is not "upside-down" on the car. Being "upside-down" is when a car owner owes more on the loan than the car is worth, and it is a frequent, yet dangerous, scenario.

New car buyers may find that buying a used car is the better option. This is especially true if it will not be driven extensively, or if a buyer wants more options and features than he or she can afford new. This is also true if the buyer knows precisely what he or she is looking for and is therefore unable to get a new car with extensive enough discounts to own it net-neutral. Used car markets are hit-or-miss. At times a car with a specific flaw can be acquired affordably. For example, an extremely low mileage used police car was for sale locally. It was never used by police forces, and was never even registered, but rather used as a demo. As a police-issue car, it had decals and an odd-array of features. For the right buyer however, this car is a steal as it offers the specific set of features in a warrantied, low mileage package for a fraction of what a "non-police" version would cost, in this case close to $10,000 less. A willing buyer can easily remove the graphics and the light bar to enjoy a car at a bargain price which they should be able to resell at a gain, owning it net-positive. This car may be an excellent alternative to a new car.

Low-mileage, late model used cars are often one of the worst investments for net-neutral or net-positive car ownership, second only to non-discounted current model new cars. Unless there is something particularly unique about the sale or the car which enables a substantial price decrease, these cars are so sought-after by car buyers that demand is driven up causing the price to become inflated, sometimes even above that of new cars. This means that for net-neutral car ownership, a car buyer must often move towards higher-mileage cars, earlier model cars, or a car with unique features or situations rendering it underpriced.

There are some unique situations that can generate underpriced cars. One situation is misplaced cars. A high end luxury car stuck in a dealership in the middle of a low-income rural town may sit there for quite a while, leading to extensive price decreases. A rear-wheel-drive sports car in snowy Syracuse, NY may do the same. In addition, a 4x4 off-road edition truck in the middle of a city might also be misplaced. These are often excellent opportunities to secure prime deals on a car. The author purchased a 4x4 off-road truck in a city for 38% off of MSRP on a new car, and bought a 6 month old 2005 model used car that sat on a used car lot for over a year in 2006 for well under market value, reselling it 2 years later for a several thousand dollar gain. The car price was dropped so far in listings that the dealer admitted after purchase that people had stopped inquiring about it, assuming something was wrong with it. Another example was when the author purchased a brand new 2006 motorcycle 3 years later in 2009. The motorcycle was still the current model, but the author was surprised to see how many people advised him "not to" buy a 3 year old new motorcycle. The motorcycle was under a new vehicle warranty and was being sold for 30% under 2006's MSRP. The same model motorcycle with no changes except color options actually increased in price by 10% over those 3 years. This means that he was actually able to purchase it for 37% off of what a new one would cost, and he even saved several thousand dollars off the cost of a used one of the same model year!

Great deals come in new and used packages. Whether it is a police car, or a mis-placed car, one that has an extremely unique option package or color, or a car that has been sitting on the lot for way too long, It is important for buyers not to count either one out too early in the buying process. Unique factors such as tax incentives, interest rate differences, and special offers can sometimes even lead a new car to be priced below a used car.

New Doesn't Always Mean New.

In reality there are actually two types of "new cars". There are simply never-before-owned cars from a dealer lot, and there are brand new to the world model cars with unique designs and features that are showing up on dealer lots for the first time. The new to the world model cars are in high demand and often have little to no flexibility in their pricing, and can actually be priced higher than MSRP! Never-before owned new vehicles may be a current model year, but these cars are no longer new unique models in high demand. For this reason, they often have good price flexibility.

It is important for any buyer to realize that acquiring a new to the world model car in high demand has a cost to it, a significant one at that. Whether or not it is worth the cost is a decision which the buyer must make based on his or her personal financial situation and emotional feelings. A buyer's dream car may be worth more to them than it is to anyone else, and as long as a buyer understands this and accepts it, such a purchase is reasonable.

In the case of buying one of these new to the world model cars, it is important to remember the basics of economics, and the traditional "supply and demand" curves. When a car first comes to market, the supply is low, and the demand is high. This drives up the price of the car, causing it to often be sold for top dollar. Since there is so much demand, a salesman knows that if a buyer does not buy the car, someone else will. Contrary to the beliefs of some buyers, this is not limited to special edition sports cars or luxury cars. Entry level cars and family sedans have the same effect when the new cars become available. Potential buyers must understand that choosing to buy at this time will make it nearly impossible to get a great deal, and certainly near impossible to end up owning the car net-neutral or net-positive. On the other hand, once a buyer determines it is worth paying a premium for the timing of the car, this does not mean there are not ways to improve the deal.

One of the prime methods of getting a better alternative deal is to look for manufacturer rebates that don't affect the bottom dollar the salesman and dealership make. This can include many of the discounts such as recent graduate discounts, military discounts, supplier pricing, or various other rebates and discounts. Another prime method is to primarily negotiate the value of a trade in car. While this may sound counterintuitive, as trade in car pricing has their limits, when purchasing a car with a strong margin, a salesman and a dealership may have clear and confined rules or decisions regarding their inability to budge on a high-demand car's pricing. On the other hand, they typically won't have such firm requirements on the trade in. While it's unlikely that the trade in value will be pushed far, if at all, above the auction value, there is a good chance that a properly negotiated trade-in should bring at least the auction value, as the dealership is making a strong margin on the car sale.

The best deals are often the ones that are tough to find. 2012 model cars in 2014 often won't even show up on some manufacturer's websites because the databases only go back two model years. The basics of "supply and demand" work both ways. As a car sits on the lot and new cars come out to take its place, the supply is higher than the demand (If demand was higher than supply, or even, the cars would have sold!) . When demand is low and supply is high, the price is driven downwards. This is precisely what opens up opportunities to receive great pricing on a new car even though it is a never-before-owned car right off the lot! Sometimes these "new" cars can even be older than two model years. A 2006 in 2009 and a 2007 in 2012 were two of the best deals ever found on new cars by this author. The concept of a "new" car truly depends on the buyer's intentions and the type of car being sought, and the buying strategy varies between the two.

Buying High Mileage

While many people are quick to recommend low mileage cars, higher mileage cars are often a great investment because their prices are much more stable. Often a car can be purchased with 85,000 to 100,000, and driven another 20-30,000 miles without significantly effecting its resale value. This can be an effective strategy for those who like to switch up cars often, as they can purchase a higher mileage car, drive it, and resell it to purchase another one when they are ready for a new car.

Mileage doesn't always correlate to condition, and in fact a car experiencing too few miles may be as problematic as those with high mileage. Many experienced buyers stay away from a car with extremely low mileage, especially older cars with low mileage. The rule of thumb is that a newer car with high mileage is better than an older car with low mileage. There are several reasons for this. First off, many parts deteriorate with age, regardless of mileage. Other parts, especially seals, belts, hoses, etc. will actually deteriorate quicker in an unused car than a car which is running, lubricating itself and building up heat to burn off carbon.

If the history of the car is known, then there can be some great lower mileage finds, but this can be tricky. A car which is only used for very short trips never gets hot enough to warm up to normal operating temperatures. While this topic is frequently debated, there are concerns about burning fuel off of cylinder walls, getting lubrication running through all moving parts, and the big one is condensation buildup in the crankcase. The one other major risk is that cars which aren't driven as much typically need more fluid changes and more care, yet owners often don't take the time to do it. The car may have been sitting for long periods of time, or has received only periodic maintenance.

It is important to address the true risks of buying higher mileage cars. The biggest risk is simply reduced resale value. The second highest risk is potential repair bills. A well-cared for car on the other hand should have relatively predictable repair bills. For many cars properly cared for, major repairs under 120,000 miles are rare. Values for the car between 95,000 and 125,000 are the same. This means buying a car with 98,000 miles in good condition may net near the same amount in resale at 123000 miles. This gives the driver 25,000 miles of driving without significantly affecting the value of the car, and with a small chance of a major repair bill. The worst case scenario on a repair bill is likely an engine or transmission, and unless the car is a high end import or unique, hard to repair car, the worst case bill will range from $1600 to $2500. Although an unlikely scenario, if this worst-case scenario were to happen, the actual "Cost" is only 10 cents a mile with the engine or transmission replacement factored in. Compare this to buying a car with 55,000 miles on it, and driving it to 80,000 miles. The depreciation alone may be $4500, which is 18 cents a mile!

Consider the difference between buying a 2007 Pontiac G5 with 119,000 miles for $6000, or a 69,000 miler for $11,000. Two separate buyers, each driving 25,000 miles, would now have 144,000 miles and 94,000 miles respectively. The prior would have a resale value of about $5200, while the latter would have a resale value of about $7,500. The first buyer would "lose" $1400 (including taxes) while the latter would "lose" $4600 (including taxes). Tack on the worst case scenario of a replacement transmission or engine. An actual replacement transmission was quoted for this car at $1200 including parts and labor, and a replacement engine was quoted at $1900. A buyer could be forced to replace BOTH the engine and the transmission, the most expensive repair parts in a scenario virtually unheard of, and would still find him or herself better off financially than buying the lower mileage alternative. There is also a good chance, if properly cared for, that the G5 would require no major service. In this case, the buyer ends up saving $3200 over buying the lower mileage alternative. Like all situations however, a well-purchased low mileage car, a poorly purchased high mileage car, or a rare car with high cost replacement parts, could alter the equation.

When pricing out repair costs, one major risk is that most ratings suggest extremely high repair costs. Once a newer model car is off of warranty, it has been around long enough to prime the used market on parts as well as spurring the development of parts by non-original equipment manufacturers (OEM). This means that the repair cost of a car drops significantly over time, often to 25% or less of the original cost. This often renders the increased price for buying lower mileage cars less likely to offer a positive return on the increased expense unless the vehicle is very high mileage (beyond warranty repair) within the first few years of its availability.

Buying cars in the 80,000-100,000 is a sweet-spot when it comes to value preservation. This is also the time when maintenance is critical, so picking a car up and giving it the "60-70k" service (or even better, getting one which recently had it completed) can help assure there are no major repairs necessary in the coming years. This may involve things such as fluid changes, water pump and thermostat replacement, and similar maintenance items. It is important to note that many cars today come with "lifetime" fluids. "Lifetime" fluids really means the lifetime of the initial buyer, and not the lifetime of the car. If the car is to be owned above 90-100k miles, many of these fluids such as differential and transmission fluids should be replaced.

Frequently there is also a lot of flexibility when buying and selling a high mileage car. A smart seller who makes sure he or she has repair and service documentation, a clean car, and a good listing can command a premium for a used car. At the same time, this smart seller may have been a smart buyer who successfully purchased the higher mileage car at a great price. If the seller is the original owner, or bought the car when it had low mileage, he or she is losing so much money relative to his or her initial purchase price, they may not pay attention to a maximizing their sale price. This gives the buyer additional negotiation room, which allows him or her to receive a better deal. The seller knows that "high mileage cars" are worth less, but they may not really know how much their car is worth. A buyer can thus negotiate a sale that allows him or her to buy the car for less than he could resell it for at that precise time period with another buyer, making net-neutral and net-positive car ownership much easier.

Many people will find it "worth the cost" to buy a car with lower mileage relieving them of the time and attention necessary to assure the car is in good shape. However, those who are looking for the best financial deal, often find higher mileage cars to be a great place for net-neutral and net-positive car ownership, especially when coupled with accurate timing of model years and desirability.

Considering Salvage and Rebuilt Cars

Salvage and rebuilt-titled cars are often regarded as the black sheep of the used car market. Buyers tend to run away from these cars, although it is not fully justified for all buyers. Salvage cars have become fairly easy to spot. They tend to be a low-mileage, good looking car that fits everything a buyer would like, but one quick glance at the price and a buyer can see that it's for a fraction of a normal car's price. The idea tempts the best of us, but we quickly move on to another car. Salvage ownership is not recommended for the casual buyer without a lot of car knowledge. For the home mechanics and automotive enthusiasts, salvage cars should be considered if it's history can be verified.

In recent years, demand for salvage cars has declined even further, and it may be due to the quick and easy manner that car history reports slap a "Do not buy" label on these cars. This trend should be moving in the other direction. Auto repair is becoming a more and more expensive business. As repair costs increase, so does the likelihood of a car being salvaged by insurance, forever branded as unwanted, even when repairable. As shop costs increase faster than inflation, new machines and equipment are needed to fix and diagnose problems, and complex manufacturing processes and complicated computer systems increase car component costs, the salvage tag becomes more and more likely.

Cars are typically listed as a total loss when the repair cost hits 70% of the cars value. While on the surface the terminology and the numbers seem to suggest a car damaged to 70% its value would not be within anyone's interest in ownership, the numbers must be put into perspective. Nada Guides (nadaguides.com), a top tier provider of car valuations, values a 1994 Geo Metro 2D Hatchback at $275 average trade in value. If an owner of this Geo Metro were to back into a light pole and scratch up the rear bumper, the paint work would cost about $350. Since $350 is more than 70% the value of the $275 car, this Geo Metro would be "Totaled" by insurance, and sold as a salvage car. For most buyers looking for a sub $1000 car, a few scratches on the rear bumper aren't going to in any way affect their ownership experience. It has no bearing on the mechanics of the car or how it works. A home mechanic or small-town shop may also decide to repaint the bumper, or pick up a replacement bumper of the same color at the junk yard, bringing the car back to its original condition. In these situations, the "salvage" title doesn't really have any bearing on the quality of the car. This if often true for cars listed as "total losses" after they are very old. It takes only minor damage for a car worth only hundreds or a few thousand dollars to exceed its value and wind up with the salvage label. Car History Reports- including the free reports available from the National Insurance Crime Bureau (NCIB.org) will tell you the date in which the car was salvaged, allowing a potential buyer to consider how much damage it would have taken to become a salvaged car.

Traditionally, older cars with a recent salvage mark were the only cars most mechanics would consider recommending. As costs increase drastically for repairing cars, even this presumption is becoming less and less true. A 2002 Maserati Spyder Convertible is listed at $24,500 low retail value according to Nada Guides (nadaguides.com) . This means that $17,000 in damage would render it in the "Total Loss" category. If this car were to slide slightly in the snow and bump into a garage door, the front bumper, a headlight, the grille, and the hood could easily be damaged. With complicated paint requirements, and insurance which agrees to get the car back to its original condition, this minor damage could cost over $17,000 due to the high retail costs for these import parts, paint, and specialty service. This could leave this very nice, perfectly functioning high end Italian sports car with the "salvage" label. A body shop or an individual home mechanic could buy this car, replace the headlight lens with a used one off ebay ($595 instead of $2560), could use a used hood ($350 instead of $3240), and a new aftermarket bumper ($260 instead of $2,570), while painting them at a local paint shop, and $17,000 in damages have been repaired perfectly for less than 10% the formal "damage" cost, leaving a completed, perfectly suitable car which had been slapped with the "salvage" label.

One other area that can leave a car with a "salvage" title even though it never saw damage is if the car was stolen for more than 30 days. After 30 days (or sooner in some jurisdictions), the car is listed as a total loss and the owner is reimbursed. If the car is later found and had no damage done to it, it still carries the "salvaged" title. Other common causes of salvage titles that may still render them fantastic cars to own are hail damage, acid rain, and external vandalism. Often these are fully repaired with no long term ramifications.

As costs continue to rise on repairing cars, this scenario will continue to become more and more prevalent, increasing the quality of cars with the "salvage" label. It is imperative to note however that any salvage cars are not what most average owners would want to deal with. Flood damage can rust a car out from the inside and lead to electrical problems which can never be solved. Cars which have damaged frames are one type of damage to stay away from for most buyers, as they may never have proper alignment, may go through tires extremely fast, and may even be unsafe.

For these reasons, purchasing "salvage" cars follow the same basic principles as entrepreneurship-Greater risk equals greater rewards. High-demand salvaged cars, fully repaired will typically cost only 60-70% the cost of the same car in a non-salvaged scenario. Low demand salvaged cars may be purchased at 50-60% of the purchase price of a non-salvaged car. This allows buyers to find cars they couldn't otherwise afford, or to get them at a better price.

Taking on this extra risk however is not for the faint of heart. Those who do not find themselves comfortable working on their own cars, who aren't interested in doing the extra research and analysis necessary, and those who aren't comfortable with car troubleshooting are typically served better by choosing to stay away from salvaged cars. They will not be able to leverage their own skill sets to cut costs, and will have a hard time lowering the risk level through research and an increase in information. For these buyers, which are the majority of casual car buyers, look for cars with minor repair items or cars that are already in good shape. Those back yard mechanics among us on the other hand, may just find these salvaged cars are well worth the risks involved, and may match themselves up with a great find at a great price.

It is essential to also note that the tradeoff in lower purchase price is that the future re-sell price will also be much lower. In addition, many buyers will not consider purchasing a salvage car, meaning they are difficult to resell, and making them very poor investment opportunities. Lowering demand almost always leads to lowering prices. For buyers looking to "flip" cars, or turn them relatively quickly for a profit or to break even, salvage cars are not good choices unless they are acquired for below salvage market values, such as below the 50% mark of the car's non-salvage value. If a buyer is planning on long term ownership with the car, has an interest in working with the car from the ground up, or finds a car they believe is in good shape and hasn't been damaged beyond efficient usage, salvage car purchases can be effective and successful.

Buyers should be wary of completely rebuilt salvage cars unless there is extensive documentation, mechanic review, and some quick calculations. Often salvage sellers say things such as "The owner backed into a wall and all that needed to be redone is a repaint of the bumper". While this may actually be true on a 1994 Geo, a 2011 Ferrari is not going to be salvaged because of a little bit of paint damage, so the numbers simply don't add up. Unrepaired salvage cars offer a lot of opportunity for buyers because they can evaluate first hand the actual damage that occurred. This allows them to see for sure what the issues are and make the repairs accordingly. Buyers can also choose what not to fix- for example, maybe a buyer doesn't need the backup camera, or they are willing to take an aftermarket bumper. Maybe a buyer can handle the rear window not working or an aftermarket exhaust. In these situations a buyer can actually save money by omitting features that aren't important to them.

One other component buyers need to be aware of when in the salvage market is that not all insurance companies will insure salvage cars, which can add a significant level of hassle and potentially some extra costs. Other insurance companies may only cover Liability insurance, and not comprehensive coverage, in which case the recently rebuilt Lotus Esprit may be covered when you hit someone else, but insurance won't be repairing your car, which may have almost as much time and money invested into it as a non-salvage car. This can be a deal-breaker for many buyers.

One last component is registration- To register a salvage car, most states have inspection requirements and inspection fees, requirements to maintain repair records and receipts, and permanent title markings illustrating that the car is salvaged. Some states also have laws requiring you to fully disclose the salvage status upon sale or be forced to pay heavy fines, which means it is important to maintain records of disclosure to your end buyer. These are additional hassles often necessary when dealing with salvage cars. Be sure to evaluate your own state's rules and procedures for Salvage Car

Ownership and Titling.

Purchasing Salvage cars is not something to recommend to most buyers, but for those who fall into the categories of home mechanics and automotive enthusiasts and know cars well, the anti-salvage sentiment that is commonplace is not necessarily the gospel so many people give creed to.

Brooks R Fiesinger

Sometimes Two is Better than One

Frequently, buyers struggle to evaluate their numerous needs in a car. They want a car with good gas mileage, but they also want to be able to haul their boat. New car types such as Hybrid SUVs suggest maybe a vehicle can meet all the needs. On the other hand, another buyer may want performance, but they also need to haul their kids around. They must determine if they should meet in the middle with a Pontiac G8, a Cadillac CTS-V, or a BMW M5. It may seem counterintuitive, but often a buyer can actually save significant amounts of money, as well as meet their goals better, by purchasing two cars instead of one. To many buyers, this may not appear viable, but once they dig deeper and consider resale, fuel economy, and insurance rates, the "two is better than one" method frequently works out.

Consider a buyer who needs to occasionally pull his or her boat from the storage location to the lake. Beyond this, he or she primarily drives long distances around the country for work. An SUV which can do both may cost $45,000 — yet they can buy a current model, low mileage used SUV for $15,000 and a nice new sedan for $25,000. Not only do they save $5,000, but the 15 MPG savings between the sedan and the SUV will pay out another $9,125 over the time this buyer owns the car, and the sedan will likely have a higher resale value than the SUV. This could save the buyer $20,000 and meet both goals better than the SUV alone.

Another analysis shows that a buyer who wants a Cadillac CTS-V may be able to meet their needs better and cheaper by purchasing two alternative brand new cars right off the dealer's floor. To balance their interest in having a Luxury Sedan to drive to and from work, for lunch meetings with clients, and to take their family on vacations with the need to have a nice sports car to zip around town in and meet their lifelong dream of owning something truly sporty, this buyer may be better off with the cheaper alternative of a CTS-V performance shattering Corvette Z06 plus an equally luxury-loaded Cadillac CTS, a BMW 328i, or an Audi A4. Getting these two new cars as opposed to a CTS-V might not only be a better fit, but it could save the buyer up to $15,000 as well. *A Detailed Analysis can be found in the appendix under Case:*

Two is Better than One.

Some buyers struggling to balance their needs among a variety of do-it-all vehicles may actually find buying two cars is better at meeting their needs than buying one. Once all factors are considered, including gas mileage, resale values, discounts, and market trends, this often becomes a better financial option as well. This allows buyers to achieve their goals more effectively and affordably.

Gas Mileage is Frequently Overrated

Many buyers hate seeing how much money it costs every time they fill up at the gas pump, but a savvy buyer knows this often does not mean they should pay a premium for specialty high-efficiency cars. While the difference of 1 Mile Per Gallon and 5 Miles Per Gallon is tremendous, as the gas mileages increase, the cost difference between two alternatives actually decreases. For example, two popular cars at the time of publication offer 42 miles per gallon and 38 miles per gallon. The 42 Miles per gallon (MPG) car costs a premium for the increased fuel economy. Many buyers however may be surprised to find that there is not much difference between the two in terms of fuel costs. While the 5 mpg car is 500% cheaper in fuel to run in than a 1 mpg car, the 42 mile per gallon car is only 10% more fuel efficient. In fact, for most "Hybrid Cars", the gas savings will never match the increased cost of the hybrid version of the car! In the scenario above between the high-mileage cars, 4 MPG may be less than $700 in fuel over the entire life of the car, which is often cheaper than the cost increase for the more efficient version.

Two other factors to consider are loan rates and a concept called "Time Value of Money" (TVM). In business this "Time Value of Money (TVM)" is an important financial concept which dictates that money is worth more today than it is tomorrow. This is the reason why banks pay interest rates, and stocks pay dividends- These companies can use money today to make more money in the future, which is then paid back to the lender in exchange for allowing them to use the money now. In other words, a dollar today is worth more than a dollar tomorrow. While in theory it does save $700 over the life of the car to go with the more fuel efficient option, This same 4 MPG is not worth paying an extra $750 or more for today, as the value of the "savings" decreases over time. If a buyer factors in loans and TVM, at 3.9% loan rate, it's not even worth paying $550 more for the 4 MPG improvement, leading many buyers to discover the hybrid and ultra-efficient versions of their cars of choice are not worth the investment.

Negotiations

Negotiation is an important part of any car purchase. It often helps buyers to plan a negotiation strategy well in advance. There is no "best way" to negotiate. This is because the best way to negotiate is always going to be the method that the seller or salesmen are not familiar with. This is known as the Buyer's Paradox. If there were a "best way" to negotiate, then the seller would likely know how to manage it and react to it, which would then mean this "best way" would lose its effectiveness.

One of the staple negotiation strategies is to simply use comparative vehicles, or to point out problems and repair costs to rationalize a lower offer price. Negotiation strategies can, however, be creative. One such method is the "non-negotiating" strategy. In other words, know how much to pay, offer this amount, and don't budge. If they don't take it, move on until someone does. There are ways to play off of this strategy in unique ways, such as via email or fax. While different forms of this "non-negotiating" strategy can be effective, they are all based on the complicated premise that a buyer needs to be extremely accurate regarding the offer calculation. Ethically, if the seller accepts, the buyer is then also obligated to complete the deal. In other words, the buyer can't use this strategy to "feel out" the seller. If the buyer is fully informed however, this can be an extremely effective strategy. It works best with dealers away from a buyer's local dealership, who have the car a buyer wants in stock, or through private party sales. It is even more effective when there is something specific which makes the deal more flexible, such as a new car which is more than two model years old, or a used car which has been sitting on the lot for months. Other strategies of varying effectiveness include asking "what's the lowest price you'll sell it for", and then offering just under it if it is within the realm of the calculated offer price. The "Irrational" approach can work as well. Most people have trouble dealing with people who lack rationality, so valuing the price on things that don't make logical sense such as offering a price based on only the options which interest a buyer and not all the options included on the vehicle, or factoring in a custom paint job, or other less rational devaluators can be effective. With some of these strategies however, if they frustrate the seller they can backfire and end any chance of acquiring the vehicle of interest.

When buying a car from a private seller, these negotiating techniques can be used, but unlike negotiating with trained salesmen, a buyer will likely be hard pressed to determine the negotiating skills of the private party seller until after they begin. Many buyers may believe that negotiations are when the two sides begin discussing money, but in fact "negotiating" has already begun the moment the parties make contact. Both parties begin to feel each other out to determine how to get the best deal. One preferred strategy when dealing with private sellers is to negotiate the price and terms before seeing the car the first time. Every time a buyer test drives the car, looks at the car, or inquires about the car, their leverage decreases. An effective strategy to prevent the loss of leverage is for a seller to negotiate a price in advance, contingent on an assumed condition which must be disclosed between the parties. When test driving the car, as long as it meets the agreed condition, the buyer purchases it.

Sometimes a buyer or seller will do what is known as a "faux deal". A faux deal is when one party believes they have a deal, but then the other party brings something unrelated to restart the negotiation process. As an example, after agreeing on terms, a woman may suggest her husband has to test drive the car before she could purchase it, or that she needs to do some more research just to make sure. When this happens it is essential that the party which believed the deal was agreed upon resists, either walking away, insisting the agreement is only valid at the current moment, or plays the same game by reneging on agreed terms for similar reasons, re-balancing the leverage.

While negotiations are an integral part of a car purchase for both new and used cars, due to the Buyer's Paradox, a specific strategy is not always effective because best practices today may not work tomorrow. Buyers are best served by being well educated on the values, pricing, and the car as a whole, to maximize their leverage. Beyond this, negotiation is more of an art than a science, but if a buyer understands their target pricing and conditions, even an unskilled negotiator can prevent themselves from running into a financial pitfall.

Remote Buying

There are a number of tools available today to purchase cars remotely in both used and new formats. From phones and faxes to the internet, where commonplace services like EBay, online auction sites, Auto trader, and even dealer's websites, remote buying opportunities are plentiful.

Most buyers today turn to the internet to do general car research, and often to find specific cars of interest. They may not realize that a significant number of buyers actually use the internet to complete an entire car purchase, and purchases are often made sight unseen.

Cars have been bought and sold remotely with great success using EBay, dealership websites, phone, fax, and forums. When done properly, buying remotely can work smoothly as long as a buyer does his homework, and negotiates effectively.

When it comes to buying new cars, a little bit of imagination can go a long way. Buying remotely can be effective for several reasons. First, it can get a buyer access to specialty cars they may not otherwise have access to, such as a brand new-yet older model year car. Manufacturer websites are often only able to inventory the current and one past model year cars. Many dealers find themselves with cars which are two or more model years old, and must access a smaller market to get rid of this less desirable car. Buying remotely can give a buyer more access to these brand new, full warranty, yet budget cars. In one case, the author was able to purchase a 2006 model when the 2010s were on the verge of coming onto the market. The vehicle was able to be purchased for 37% off of the price of the new 2010 versions, yet was brand new with a full warranty. Some people don't realize that most manufacturers' warranties do not begin until the car is purchased. This means that if a buyer purchases a 2006 car in 2009, the warranty period still lasts the full time-period after purchase.

A second major benefit to buying new cars remotely is that a buyer can maintain significantly more leverage than they can in a local, in-person scenario. Since it is easier to "walk away" and buy from someone else, it takes less of an investment from a buyer's perspective to consider the purchase. It also offers less investment of time and money from a seller's perspective, allowing him or her to sell at a lower price. In 2010 when the author decided to purchase a brand new 2010 Camaro SS, since the car was new and in demand, the local dealer would not offer any amount off the purchase price. Upon looking up another dealer that had the same car the author wanted, he completed research on the salespeople before contacting them. He found the youngest, least experienced salesman because they were likely to be excited about the sale and most likely willing to take the smallest commission. He then sent them an email and essentially said- "If you will give me the car for [X amount], and agree to give me [X amount] for my trade in, let me know and I can be up there today to complete the transaction". A few hours later he received a phone call where the salesman said "I'm just calling to find out if this email offer I received today was legitimate or not?". After confirming that it was, he checked with the sales manager and got a few minutes later with an offer acceptance. He drove several hours to the remote dealership later that day and picked up the car. All said and done, buying remotely saved thousands of dollars.

By taking the purchase to a larger group of sellers, the basic principle of supply and demand is demonstrated. As the supply of sellers increases for the same demand, prices will fall, often leading the buyer to get a better deal by being able to get business from the dealers who are competing with each other for your business. A larger pool of options also opens up the chances of finding a specific car that a dealer may be more eager to get rid of, possibly because they have excess inventory, or one which has only the features and components a buyer is seeking. When looking for a truck, the author was able to look at dealers within a several hundred mile radius to determine who had significant excess inventory of the prior year models on the type of truck that he sought. The author was able to contact several dealerships about how low they could go, see if they could match or beat each other, and ultimately was able to get two trucks down to $12,000 to $14,000 off or MSRP.

The big negative of buying a new car remotely is that it means a buyer won't have the opportunity to test drive or view the actual car they will be purchasing. If a buyer has done enough research however, and is familiar with the cars, there likely won't be any surprises. The cars come with a full warranty, so if anything is wrong with them they will be repaired, and on a new car, there are rarely any significant concerns regarding potential damage or vehicular condition. The fear of buying a new car sight unseen is largely irrational, and great deals can be achieved by making this sacrifice.

When it comes to used cars, with risk comes reward, and with no risk there is no reward. One key to a smart purchase is to find where the rest of the market actually bears more risk than a specific buyer would. An example would be a seller offering a car on EBay to the entire country, yet where the listing is local allowing a specific buyer to investigate the car before bidding. In these situations, while the price of a car is based on market risk with most buyers being forced to buy sight-unseen, the buyer is getting a better deal because they are not taking the same risk to acquire the car. Remote buying is best optimized for rare cars, specialty cars, and specialty conditions, but some buyers may turn to remote purchasing for general car purchases as well.

Finding a scenario where the market bears more risk than a specific buyer is often accomplished by doing significant research, such as investigating what the car problems are and how easy they are to solve, to determine quirks about specific model years or option packages, or by evaluating unique market situations. When a buyer chooses to purchase remotely, it can often be very difficult bear less risk than the rest of the market. It is possible when a buyer becomes an expert on specific models or car types. In these scenarios, the market forces will keep the cost of the car low (higher risk remote purchase), but since the buyer has more information than the market, or they can check the car out themselves the buyer is lowering their own risk, but not effecting the big picture market risk.

For the vast majority of situations however, it is difficult to know more than the market does when buying used cars remotely. There are a few tricks and opportunities which are fairly low risk that buyers can take to get both a great deal, and a safe deal.

If a buyer resides in a city, he or she will note that used car prices tend to be higher, as there are many more customers for a seller. More demand leads to higher prices. On the other hand, off into the country, buyers can be rare, especially for less mainstream cars like collector's cars, 2 seater roadsters, and sports cars. This means sellers must compensate with lower prices. When purchasing a Mercedes SLK Convertible, the author was able to find a seller 2 hours away, far from any cities or large towns who had the car listed for quite a while. He was able to email the seller a fairly low offer, which was accepted. Remote buyers should consider, when possible, including a clause that the "offer is only valid if the car is truly in the condition it appears to be in by your description". The author was able to give the car a good look-over, determine that it was in the condition described, and was able to pay and get on his way. Less-savvy sellers can also take the car to a mechanic to confirm the condition before paying what they offered. A used truck bought remotely had been driven for only 5 months, and then traded in to a dealership. The dealership had the car sitting almost two years, a long time for a used car dealership, and had consistently dropped the price to the point where many buyers would have thought the title was salvage or there was major damage to it, as it was priced far under market value. The truck was taken to a mechanic who was able to confirm its condition. It was still under warranty. The seller was paid, and the buyer had a great truck in hand.

Buyers do at times have to walk away after agreeing to a remote sale. When this happens, they are glad they had that quality and performance clause in the offer so they could. In one instance, a 1977 Camaro Z28 looked great in the pictures, and the seller touted how great the condition was, but the car was extremely rusty and painted over with spray paint. Serious fluid leaks were also evident in the engine bay, rust had eaten up the rear end, and the car was over-all far from the condition as portrayed.

While most remote buyer situations can be conditional on the car meeting quality and performance expectations, at times cars must be purchased without that benefit, such as purchasing from Ebay. These purchase decisions and situations are much more complex, and for buyers looking for a reliable commuter car for a single car situation, or for someone without a lot of car knowledge, the risk in these scenarios will typically outweigh the potential reward. For those looking for a second or third car, a collectors car, a project, or are extremely car savvy, this remote buying situation can be extremely rewarding.

When buying used cars remotely on Ebay, another website, a collector car catalog, or something similar and the car is being shipped to you, the sale can become quite a bit trickier. When it is not possible to test drive or evaluate the car ahead of time, and a buyer cannot include a clause based on its condition, it is often "buyer beware". Although there is an increased risk, good deals are often had in these situations. Only purchase remotely in this situation when the extra risk is reflected in a significantly lower price, and be mentally prepared for potential blemishes, scratches, minor damage, and minor problems not evident in the pictures and descriptions. The important thing however is to maximize the amount of acquired information to minimize the associated risk in purchase.

A buyer can lower risk by getting as much detail as possible in writing, as well as photos and additional documentation. While they will be locked into the purchase, if there is clear fraud (where the buyer explicitly states something in writing with intent of deceiving a buyer), there are still legal ramifications which can be taken to receive recourse. The Federal Magnuson-Moss Warranty Act was enacted in 1975, and permits buyers to file legal actions against warranties including implied warranties and service contracts. On the other hand, buying cars from a private party are typically not covered by the Federal Trade Commission's used car disclosure rules or state disclosure and implied warranty rules, and are presumed "as-is" unless explicitly stated otherwise in writing. If a legitimate case is anticipated, buyers can opt to go to small claims court, or in the case of the purchase being through a legitimate franchised dealer, a seller may be able to contact AUTOCAP (Automotive Consumer Action Program) run by the National Automotive Dealers Association for mediation. [1] Beware that when filing a small claims court dispute, it may have to be filed in the location where the purchase or transaction was made, which means in the case of a remote purchase, a buyer may have to travel to the location of purchase. Be sure to consult an attorney regarding legal actions, procedures, and limitations in your state, as every case is different, and be sure to keep as many records as possible.

Buyers will often find it very worthwhile to run a VIN number check to unearth anything that could be hiding, and consider having a local mechanic check it out even if a buyer cannot. This can often be had for under $200. We recommend simply calling a local mechanic who has solid reviews through review channels such as Angie's list (angieslist.com) or online review boards. Alternatively, services such as inspectmyride.com allow a buyer to set up a car inspection remotely for under $200. These types of inspections are not only good advice for any purchase decision, but when purchasing remotely they can give a buyer substantial information about the condition of the car they are buying.

Other specific questions that should be asked is for accident history, title status, questions about specific concerns unique to the car make or model, and for additional pictures of any damage or problem areas. A buyer can also request receipts for any repair work, measurements of tire tread or brake pad life, and shipping information. Buyers can often contact repair shops directly which have done repair or customization work on the car to double check statements. Buyers are strongly encouraged to get as much of this information as possible in writing, such as via email, or by requesting a disclosure sheet mailed or faxed. Verbal information, while helping to get a feel for its condition, will typically be impossible to use in the case of litigation or evaluation. Because of this, sellers will likely be reluctant to mislead or misrepresent in writing, while verbally they may lead you to believe a car is in better condition than it is.

There are significant additional precautions that should be made when purchasing remotely. Even if the vin check returns positive information, beware if the car is being sold in an area that recently saw flood damage, hail damage, or hurricane damage, as this can often be difficult to diagnose from a distance. If the car has been in a significant accident, evaluate the pricing based on the worst case scenario. Above all other precautions, never take the sellers word for anything with the car. Most sellers are honest sellers who intend to give you accurate information, but many sellers have limited vehicular knowledge. The author had one seller who insisted her car was a V-8 even as he was standing over the engine bay counting the cylinders for her. In this case she simply didn't know any better.

When done properly, by limiting the amount of risk taken in remote car purchases, buyers can get an excellent deal on the car they want. These cars can be had for a fraction of a local purchase, and special or unique cars are more readily available when a buyer is looking for something specific. This includes unique color combinations, rare editions, or certain setups. For collector cars, this also often means low mileage and cars from south of the road-salt line. Unless it has been explicitly cared for as a collector's car, buyers must expect significant undisclosed minor issues such as wear and paint issues. For most buyers this is not a deal breaker, but by being prepared in advance, keeping this in mind will allow buyers to enjoy their new car to its full potential.

The Dealer

Contrary to the opinion of some car buyers, the salesperson is not evil. The salesperson is simply trying to make money just like the buyer does in his or her career. They make money by selling cars. The more they are invested in the sale, the more they will expect to be compensated for their efforts. Younger salespeople with less experience will often take lower cuts for themselves. Buying without taking up their time also lowers their investment in completing the sale. While it may be suggested on website forums, do not keep the salespeople "after hours". This is actually increasing the seller's investment in the sale, leading them to ultimately demand more from the buyer in compensation for their time.

It is important to recognize that the salesman and the dealer need to feed their families too. A buyer cannot expect to get a car so cheap that the dealership doesn't make money, and the salesman does not get a paycheck. For this reason it is important to have realistic expectations of the buying experience, while still maximizing leverage. Every time a buyer asks questions, requires interactions, or test drives cars; it has a "cost" added to your car purchase.

It is often helpful to see things from the dealer's perspective. While it may seem smart to a buyer to visit while it's raining because they feel there won't be many others shopping, a car salesman may see it differently. The seller will assume the buyer must be pretty desperate to come out on a day with miserable weather, weakening the buyer's leverage.

Understanding Dealer Floor Plans:

Dealers typically don't own their entire inventory, and instead use a lender to finance the inventory. This means they have to pay interest on their inventory each month. The typical interest rate for a Floor Plan loan is about 4-5% over prime, so if prime is 5.5%, the interest rate for the dealer may be 10%. This means that a $25,000 car on the lot may cost the dealer $2,500-2,618 a year in interest alone, or $208-218 a month. This means the seller has a "holding cost" of over $200 a month, which motivates them to sell prior to the end of the month, and offers leverage to the buyer.

When should a Dealer be visited?

One topic debated frequently in the realm of car purchasing is the topic of when is the best time to purchase a car. Unfortunately, like most other areas involved with car purchasing, there is no single hard and fast rule, as every company, dealership, and model all have factors which influence the timings. There are however a number of time periods worth evaluating and monitoring to maximize prime purchase timing opportunities to achieve the best pricing.

Purchasing at the end of the year and the end of the month tend to be good times to buy. Car salespeople and dealerships both typically have quotas which they have to meet to achieve revenue goals and often payments from the manufacturers. A quota is a certain number of cars or dollar amount of cars necessary for a salesperson or a dealership to sell within a certain time period, typically monthly or yearly. The end of the month and the end of the year are often both great times to buy because both salespeople and dealers often have to meet these quotas.

While the end of the year is often a great time to buy a new car, buyers are frequently deceived as they fail to recognize that the end of the fiscal year for the company is often not the end of the calendar year. The Internal Revenue Service accepts the Generally Accepted Accounting Principles (GAAP) and allows for fiscal years either at the end of the calendar year or at the end of a chosen fiscal year which may end at a different time period. While they can change, at the time of this publishing, the Chrysler, Hyundai, Volkswagen, and Ford Fiscal Years end December 31st. General Motors ends December 30th. Toyota and Nissan on the other hand end March 31st, while Honda's fiscal year ends on March 30th. Specific dealership's fiscal years are also permitted to vary, and while many will be the end of the calendar year, or in line with their respective manufacturers, others vary throughout the year. Many dealers do correspond with their manufacturer counterparts, although others have strategically found it beneficial to maintain a timeline of their own. To further complicate this purchasing timing, buyers will often find that the last day of the month is not the true last day. Dealers often flex into several days (typically up to 3) past the month and the year to still meet quotas and maintain allocation and incentive demands, as well as grace periods for their own floor plan financing.

Midweek purchasing can be beneficial. While the ultimate buying strategy should be determined in advance, for those looking to show up at a dealership and complete a sale in person, Tuesdays and Wednesdays are the slowest days at the lot. This not only offers dedicated time to work with a salesman and less hassle dealing with a number of other people at the dealership, but it also lowers the perceived value of the salesman's time, lowering their perceived investment in the sale. This is especially important for buyers who choose to take a long time to consider a car purchase. Visiting on a Tuesday or Wednesday can help prevent the salesman from artificially and subtly, possibly even without their conscious knowledge, demanding more to compensate for their efforts.

Visit at the end of the month, avoiding the beginning of the month. Typically, rebates and incentives are not published on the first of the month, but instead are typically published on the early side of mid-month. Showing up the first few days often means a buyer will lose out on that month's deals, as well as the last month's deals which have already expired. These deals are typically offered from the manufacturer, which means the additional money off does not affect the dealership's bottom line.

Consider shopping on holidays. Contrary to popular opinion, holidays are often down times without significant traffic at the dealership. Days before and after on the other hand, may see increased traffic. During these holidays, there are often significant manufacturer rebates and special offers available. This makes holidays a good time to buy.

When considering what time of day to visit the dealership, early is better than late. It is not an effective strategy to try to catch the salesperson late in the day, even though many buyers falsely assume they will get a better deal by inconveniencing and putting pressure on the salesman. It is probably safe to say that most people do not like to be kept at work late without advanced notice. By forcing these salespeople to stay late, buyers have actually increased the seller's investment in the sale, which will ultimately leave them determined to maximize their compensation for their sacrifices. Instead, Early in the day is often better than late in the day. Salespeople would love to get the day started with a sale. There is also the added benefit of there being fewer customers at the dealership!

There are a number of variables to consider when determining the best timing for purchasing a car. Buyers need to evaluate available incentives with their buying strategies and the fiscal calendar years of the dealerships. In addition, buyers must evaluate the lifecycle of the cars themselves (new models will have less available incentives no matter what time of year they are unveiled), as well as the timing in the month, the day of the week, and the time of day they choose to purchase. By evaluating these perspectives together, a buyer can maximize their opportunities to get the best pricing for their purchasing decision.

Used Cars from Dealers:

Used cars from a dealer are difficult to determine the best pricing in advance, as there is no way to determine what the dealer paid. At the same time, used dealers tend to operate at significantly higher margins than new car dealers, allowing them a little more wiggle room. There are certainly guides a buyer can use to help determine a value for the cars they are interested in, but all too often the pricing guides are significantly off. As a seller, the author has frequently dealt with buyers who say things such as "The book value is $14,500 so that is all I'll pay", when the seller knows the car is worth $18,500. As a seller, he kindly turns these people away and they never really understand why, leaving them searching for a car "for a fair price" for a long time, never finding something in the right condition at what they believe is fair price based on the guides. The issue in this real scenario is not that the sellers are asking too much for their cars, but rather the buyer has put too much weight on a guidebook. In 2010-2012, if the author could find a Corvette for book value, he would have bought them all up to just resell, as they were all actually selling for prices sometimes close to double the "book value".

Since the "book value" for a car cannot be relied upon wholly, it is important for a buyer to determine what the true value of a car is. Whether a buyer is buying from a dealer or a private party, the best way to do this is by doing homework. Determine at what price sellers are listing a car for, and how much they are likely selling them for. A sub $5000 car will normally sell for about $500 less than list price with many exceptions. $5000-$11000 cars frequently sell for about $800-$1200 less. Cars priced higher than $11,000 frequently find themselves going for $1,000 to sometimes as high as several thousand less than listing prices. Since these are largely private party prices being evaluated, it is important to then factor in that the used car dealer has to make a profit. It is common to normally factor in 5-7% more from a dealer, as a buyer should safely presume they bought it for 7-15%

less than market value (or at auction value). They also may have had to make minor fixes and repairs plus detail and prep the car (5%). Tack on administrative costs and holding costs (4%), and then a fair profit margin (6%). Auction prices are often as much as 15% lower than retail prices, but higher volume dealerships will pick up easy to move cars closer to 7% under retail. Buy here, pay here lots are often priced well over 25% the typical retail prices. Sometimes cars will take more prep work, sometimes less, and as a buyer there is no way to know what they paid for it or had to invest in it to know what they need for a profit.

The potential fluctuations in a dealer's willingness to let the car go at acceptable prices means that a buyer is much more likely to simply have to "walk away" from a used car. If the dealer paid $6500 for a car, and is selling it for $8500, and a buyer offers $6400, they won't take it. Take the same car where the dealer pays $5100 for it, and is selling it for $7500. You offer the same $6400, and there is a much greater chance that they will accept the offer. Typically when buying from auctions, dealerships have no way to judge the quality of the car in the ways in which a buyer can, which means sometimes dealerships pay over what they should for some cars, and in other cases, they pay less.

Used car buyers must take a market-based approach to purchasing instead of a cost-based approach to purchasing. It is essential to discover what the car is "worth", and work towards finding a version of the car a buyer wants that can be found for slightly less than this valuation. To maximize your investment, it is best for buyers to take a big-picture objective look at the car market, and to consider cars which are either unlikely to depreciate, or those which may actually appreciate. To get the best deals, buyers should look for cars with something minor that is wrong. As an example, a buyer bought a Mazda 3 that was in great shape, but had warped rear rotors. On a test drive, the buyer could feel how warped they were, causing the car to shake. To confirm, the warped shape could be felt with the buyer's hand during inspection. The market value of the car at the time was around $8,500. He knew other people who test drove the car would walk away because of the shaking. In order to only buy cars at great prices, the buyer offered the sellers $6,200 for it, knowing it was less than they wanted, and told the sellers to call him if they were unable to sell it for more. As expected, several hours later they received a phone call stating they'd take $6,600. $70 in rotors later (and 1 replacement used tire which was $55), the buyer has a car which would easily fetch $8,500 in the market, and yet was only in it for $7200- including repairs, tax, title, and plates! This means after driving it for a year or two, the used car market on Mazda 3s dropped only slightly, allowing it to be sold for approximately $7400 making a slight profit and getting a few years of usage out of it!

Other cars in this category of minor repairs included a Mercedes SLK with a non-working roof ($17 for the repair seals, easily fixed at home or at a repair shop!), a Mercedes which had a blown fan relay fuse ($2.80 repair cost that took less than a minute), a Yamaha Motorcycle that needed a new brake pedal ($96 at the dealer), and an Isuzu that needed a new ground cable ($4.80 and 5 minutes of time). The key business principle is straight forward. It remains the basic concept of supply and demand. As demand for a car drops, its market value drops. Problems lower the demand for the car, in turn lowering its value.

Demand-Based Purchasing:

Most buyers are simply looking for any reason not to buy a car, as opposed to looking at problems as "reduced value". Imagine taking this same approach in buying a house: Will a buyer eliminate a house because they don't like just one single light fixture, or because it needs new door locks? This would be highly unlikely. If the house needs a new roof after inspection, buyers typically don't just walk away - instead they ask for $8,000 off the purchase price since they now have to replace the roof. Smart buyers look at car buying the same way. While the neophyte should certainly stay away from complex problems and major unknowns, minor and simple "issues" can allow a car to be purchased at a much lower cost, and a quick call to a repair shop (or dropping off the car yourself for a look over) could unveil the repair costs. The risk is often worth the significant reward. One thing no buyer should ever do however is "trust" the seller. Even if the seller is talking about the problems in good faith, if it really was a "$20 fix that takes 10 minutes", they would have already completed it.

Buy Here, Pay Here Dealerships:

When a buyer is looking for a car, but has too little cash to purchase a car directly and has a poor credit rating and cannot get financing elsewhere, he or she may find themself at a dealership offering "Buy Here, Pay Here" services. Buy Here, Pay Here services are dealerships offering cars to the least creditworthy buyers by financing them directly. For those with strong credit who are interested in a car at a buy here, pay here dealership, typically it is advantageous to bring in outside financing at a lower interest rate, such as from a bank or credit union. When paying in cash, buyers can often get a great deal, but it may be difficult to find a salesman to work with effectively due to the dealership's income structure.

To understand why buy-here pay-here lots rarely lead to a good financial deal for the buyer, it is important to understand how they work. While specific strategies may differ slightly from one lot to another, the basic premise of selling to someone who isn't credit worthy is to minimize risk and maximize reward. Based on interviews with several owners of Buy-Here, Pay-Here lots, a dealer will sell the car with a down-payment high enough to pay the dealers actual cost for the car so that even if they never find a buyer again, they still didn't lose money. Some dealers often also count on a buyer missing payments so the dealer can repossess the car and resell it, essentially getting multiple sales per car. Those who do come through with their payments sometimes can end up paying well over three or four times the car's true market value leaving them with a big expense with a small asset remaining. Interest rates often start at around fifteen percent and average about twenty percent, but can be as high as thirty-five percent. While these rates sound high, they are often masked by weekly or biweekly payment plans. According to an article by CNNMoney, repossession rates are typically close to twenty-percent.[3]

Dealers determine how much money per week the potential buyer makes, and arranges payments based on this pay schedule. He or she helps the buyer identify the cars they can afford. Since the first step is customized on how much the buyer can afford, there is typically no real room for negotiations or price comparisons. Once a potential buyer sees how these lots work, it quickly becomes evident that there is no way to negotiate a good deal or to receive a good deal.

Often buyers are individuals attempting to rebuild their credit, or who simply cannot get a loan at a traditional institution. It is strongly recommended that anyone who finds themselves in this situation to take a step back to consider the big picture. Instead of getting a large loan to drive a car worth much less, potential buy-here pay-here customers should consider searching for a really low priced car for short term usage. Car purchases under five-hundred dollars are available. While many of these cars are far from tip top shape, they are often cheaper than a down-payment on a car at a buy-here, pay here lot. Additionally, since these cars are so low priced to start with, they tend to retain their value, allowing an owner to "upgrade" quickly with the money they are saving, without having to endure the financial loss and high risk associated with making car payments on a car worth less than they are paying.

If a buy-here, pay-here lot was going to charge a buyer $50 a week, and a buyer can manage on an ultra-budget car for just 3 months, the potential buyer would have an extra $600 available to spend on a car. Save a little more each month out of a paycheck, and a buyer can soon buy a reliable car, albeit an older car. Once a more reliable car is purchased, the money that would have been going to a dealership can then go towards future repairs and an even newer car in the coming months, building wealth and stability for the individual's future.

If a potential buyer is looking to purchase from a buy-here pay-here lot, there are a few areas they should research before putting their name on the end of that contract. These are areas which often won't apply to buyers of other traditional financing and car purchases. These include confirmation that the dealership will report your positive payment history to the credit bureaus, the payment policies, guarantees and payment plans available at the dealership, and what payment methods are acceptable. Often buy-here pay-here lots require in-person checks or cash at their dealership. If a buyer lives a good distance from the dealership, this could be a concern.

Many advocates of buy-here-pay-here lots will point out some of the arguable benefits of buy-here pay-here lots- cheap cars, credit for those who can't afford otherwise, and sometimes service plans and decent warranties. There is an extremely high "cost" attached to this type of service which savvy buyers can bypass with a little bit of creativity, hard work, and dedication. While there are always exceptions to every rule, shy away from against buy-here, pay-here lots for most buying situations.

Used Cars from Private Sellers

Working with Private Sellers is significantly different from buying from dealerships. The dynamics in the situation are completely changed, and therefore buying behavior must change also. These private sellers are often emotionally attached to their cars, overvalue their cars, are frequently lacking knowledge about their cars, and are often unsure of themselves when they sell a car, giving a buyer who knows what they are doing, a tremendous amount of positive leverage.

When sellers have owned the car they are selling, often for an extended amount of time, they naturally become attached to it. This means that not only are they making a financial deal, but they are giving something up that has value to them. This has several effects. Primarily, consumers always over-value what they have and undervalue what someone else has. This is true in the automotive market as well as virtually every other buying and selling market. Sellers will overlook issues the car has, and over-evaluate features, fixes, or additions when setting prices for their car. Sometimes they have such an inflated view of their car's value that a sale simply won't happen until they begin to get more desperate to sell. This often creates a windfall fire sale price to the eventual buyer, but to early buyers, the seller will hold fast. In these cases, buyers should walk away or plan on making a deal in the future.

A second effect private sellers have from their natural attachment to their car is that the buyer needs to feel good about the sale, just like the buyer does. This means a buyer can often make a lot of headway by complimenting the car, which is counterintuitive for most buyers. By offering them more than money for the car, such as emotional support and affirmation, a buyer can often get a great deal. Sellers feel better selling to someone they feel they can trust, that will care for their car, and that will continue to love the car. Making the seller believe that the car buyer will be a good future owner who will take care of it can in many cases help the seller part with it at a lower final price.

One last effect is that when a private seller sells a car, they are consumed by the sale. They will think about it until the car is sold. If the seller overpriced their car, the car will likely have few potential buyers. If it has been on the market long enough that they are getting nervous/desperate, they will be afraid there aren't buyers out there and will be afraid of losing the sale. Instead of logically dropping the price slightly, they will often take a low ball offer, especially if it is properly handled. While a dealership may move on to another customer, this seller will play "What if" scenarios over and over in their heads. As a buyer, the author has often found cars he was interested in. Noting how long the car has been on the market, and knowing it won't sell close to the price listed, he will wait weeks, even months, before offering a significantly lower offer, which is often accepted as the buyer has then begun to get incredibly nervous. When a potential buyer actually buys from a private seller is often a significant factor.

Savvy buyers should use this to their benefit, and offer a low ball offer. Rationally explain to the seller why the low ball offer is fair, and let them know there are other potential cars in the mix. Let the seller know that they can contact you if they can't find a willing buyer within a deadline of a few days to a week, or "As long as you haven't bought another car already". To play this strategy well, they need to know the buyer is going and test driving other cars as soon as they leave! The seller will then start to look at the worst case scenarios once the potential buyer has departed, and will often call the potential buyer back quickly. It can also be effective sight-unseen. Some buyers won't get any or many inquiries, so a quick email that says "I can offer X amount and here's why, call me if you're interested," may spark his or her interest. When offering sight unseen however, be sure to throw a conditional in there, such as "Assuming it is of the condition it appears to be in by your listing".

It is important for buyers to be confident when purchasing from private sellers, as the seller is typically not. The car sale decision and process is a relatively rare occurrence for private sellers, and therefore they are not experts at it. Any time a buyer offers them an amount, the buyer should explain why they are offering that amount so it makes sense to the seller. Confidence, rationality, and research will normally give the buyer the upper hand in negotiations, and often it is not difficult to exceed the knowledge of the seller both on the sales process and on understanding their car. Using comparables that a buyer has looked at elsewhere (either online or in person), deducting repair costs for specific needs, and dropping the offer for "unknowns" (such as something "may be" a brake pad or a transmission) is an effective way to justify the offer. For an example, the repair cost for a Mercedes SLK Convertible top was between $3200 and $3800 depending on the dealership and repair shop quoted, yet a $17 seal kit off of a popular SLK Web Forums can make the same repair. This high cost can significantly lower the purchase price of the car, and can be lucrative as a net-positive purchasing opportunity for buyers, especially for quick fixes. A buyer can also justify price influences with market information and other concerns which the seller can acknowledge, such as a new version of the car coming out, high mileage, tire or brake replacement coming soon, or reliability concerns from reliability reports. Forums are also a great tool for finding potential issues on cars, which a buyer can use as part of their negotiation tactics. The author was able able to get $4200 knocked off of a used Nissan Xterra a few years ago by citing legitimate common repair costs that often begin to emerge about the same mileage as the car, even though the car wasn't exhibiting those issues at the time of purchase!

Like in other areas of buying and selling cars, it is very important not to lie, cheat, or act unethically. There is plenty of opportunity to get great deals without reverting to questionable ethics. While some people do choose to act unethically when buying and selling cars, it can catch up with them. Everything has a cost, and while a few dollars may be saved or earned with unethical car dealings, for the vast majority of people, the ethical cost exceeds the financial reward many times over, and it taxes society at large as well. Buyers and Sellers alike will be more satisfied with themselves when legitimately and ethically getting a great deal on their purchase or sale.

Many sellers also don't realize that car loans are now readily available for private party sales. While rare in years past, most banks and credit unions now allow buyers to purchase a used car from a private party. If a buyer plans to go this route, make certain to be pre-approved for cars in the expected price range ahead of time. Secondly, be sure not to let the seller know the purchase will be financed through a bank until the two parties have already agreed on a price. While it may not seem like a big deal to the buyer, it opens up the possibility of losing significant leverage. A smart seller knows that if a buyer is choosing to finance a car, it becomes a lot easier to convince the buyer to pay a little more money. In addition to this, a seller may actually consider the potential buyer with a loan less of a quality buying candidate than a cash sale. Whether accurate or not, most sellers live by the thought that "cash is king". Fortunately when a buyer's bank or credit union finances the sale, the seller will get the cash (or bank check) in hand, making it ultimately the same outcome to them as a cash sale. It will require more effort on the seller's behalf, as they will likely have to travel to the bank offering the loan, and will have to complete additional paperwork. Just like on new cars and car dealerships, when a private party must do more work and deal with more hassle, they will feel they must be compensated for the time which will be reflected from the price demands during the negotiation process.

There are other caveats regarding car loans on private party purchases. Beware of repair costs. On a private purchase, there is rarely an existing warranty unless the car is only a couple of years old. If there is an existing warranty, some manufacturers do not have fully transferrable warranties, and even if it does transfer, it is likely shorter than the loan payoff period. This means that to be able to afford the car, the buyer also needs to be able to afford the repair costs, which could be several thousand dollars in the case of a major repair to the engine or transmission. It is also important for the seller to maintain positive equity during the loan in case there is any reason to sell it.

When buying from private parties, a buyer's logic may be deceiving. A simple case study can be found by visiting a grocery store. If a buyer were to calculate the "per ounce" cost of Ketchup between the large family size package and the small bottle, many buyers are surprised to notice the "family size" package is more expensive per ounce than the small bottles! This is largely because marketers are intelligent, and once they realized that buyers started assuming "bulk" is cheaper per ounce, they knew those buyers wouldn't continue to price check on many of their standard purchases, and stick with their initial logic. For this reason, marketers will often mix it up and raise the price on the products which consumers "assume" are the lowest price! As time goes on and consumers as a whole adapt and change their behavior, the marketers will respond and change theirs At the time of this writing, bulk and family size ketchup is more expensive than the small bottles. Once the average consumer figures this out, the marketers will have to adapt to this changing consumer behavior. This means that the buying process and negotiation tactics will likely differ from past car purchases. The seller's strategy will always be to out think the buyer's logic during car sales, and will switch their strategies as buyers get used to the old sales strategies. This is just like marketers changing the pricing of the ketchup as consumers caught on to the old pricing strategies, even if it seems to defy logic to the buyer on the surface.

The specific problem is that buying is simply game-theory in action. Each party will try to figure out what the other party is trying to do, and figure out how they can influence the other party in their favor. This means there are often counterintuitive behaviors going on. Consider Game Theory merged with basic Supply and Demand. During winter, about a month before the weather improves, sellers can often get top dollar for their convertible sports cars. As the weather warms up, the markets will see a short term flooding of these sports cars as many sellers attempt to get top-dollar for their car. Each seller undercuts the existing market, trying to sell quickly before the buyers buy up other cars. The current sellers respond by lowering their prices, driving prices to rock bottom for a few short weeks until supply starts selling and more demand emerges. This means a buyer can actually get a great price on a convertible right as summer begins, and get a great deal on a 4x4 SUV right as winter is on the horizon, even though this is counterintuitive to most buyers initial logic. When a buyer considers the seller's behavior and thought process on the other hand, they can use that behavior to their benefit in acquiring a good price for the car they want.

Mechanics and Car Reports

A very basic Car Identification Number (VIN) check is available for free at NCIB.org. The National Insurance Crime Bureau will tell you if there is a theft record for the car or if the VIN has been reported as a total loss, as well as the date of the total loss and the reason. If a seller chooses not to do an entire VIN check, this can be a free way to help determine if the title is clean. This free report doesn't offer service records or detailed car information as these are only available for paid services. Paid services are available at a variety of costs, from $2.50 for limited searches, to $55 or more for complete information. Two services dominate the more expensive reports, Carfax.com, the market leader, and Autocheck.com, powered by Experian. Based on an independent study in 2013 with various VINS of different years and makes, Autocheck.com reported more records than Carfax did, although at times Carfax contained information Autocheck was missing. At the time of this publishing, Autocheck was cheaper than CarFax. Buyers should consider purchasing the unlimited reports from either provider, as the reports may turn up information that makes a deal breaker, may turn up information a buyer can use for added negotiation, or can even provide some information that makes a car significantly more appealing. They are best used not only at the final decision making stage, but also in the negotiation and investigation phases. For example, when looking to buy a Maserati, the author knew that the clutches needed to be replaced every 18,000 to 21,000 miles, at a cost of $3500 to $5000. When Carfax reported that the clutch was replaced just about a thousand miles ago, the author knew this common maintenance item wouldn't be needed, increasing the value of the car to him as a buyer.

Cheaper alternatives, such as Instavin.com are also available. While some of the cheapest options simply share the same information as the free National Insurance Crime Bureau resource above, mid range options such as Instavin fall in the $7-12 range and offer a lot of great information about your car, as well as covering most of the more important items buyers tend to be looking for. These reports are often less complete than AutoCheck or CarFax, and do not offer an unlimited option, meaning in most buying scenarios it can actually be cheaper to go with AutoCheck or CarFax. On the other hand, if a buyer is simply trying to verify information, gauge the seller, or check for specific facts likely to be found on Instavin such as the number of owners or usage over time, Instavin.com is a great resource.

Deciding not to acquire this information can lead to a more expensive outcome for the buyer. These searches are not however limited to checking for a "clean title," as a buyer typically can either use it in negotiations for a lower price, or will feel more confident in their car ownership. In addition, by printing out the report (or saving it on a computer), a buyer can actually increase the sales price and negotiating power when they sell their car, by sharing it with prospective buyers. Buyers often wait too long in the buying process to check the report after they have already made the purchase decision. At this time they have already lost buying leverage, and are unable to use the resource to aid in the purchase and negotiation decision.

Do keep in mind that Carfax.com, Autocheck.com, and the alternatives are simply tools. They do not always tell the entire story, and should not be relied upon wholly on their own. Cars which have been significantly damaged are not always reported if the body shop doesn't report it, or if the car owner repairs the car themselves. In addition, many properly serviced cars are also never reported meaning there's often a lot of the story, both positive and negative, which is simply not supplied in these reports. They do help fill in some of the gaps, and the data which is shared can be extremely helpful.

A common recommendation is having a mechanic check over a car for a buyer, yet most buyers never do have this check completed. An alternative for most individuals is to find a friend or neighbor who is much more car savvy than they are, and who may be able to judge the car better than they can. Many home mechanics can quickly spot when something isn't right, and can troubleshoot common problems. If something seems fishy, confusing, or a problem isn't easily determined, then a trip to a mechanic is warranted. In the purchase decision process, it is reasonable to have a mechanic review the car after the deal is reached, with the mechanic being used as a contingency. As a buyer, it is often wise when there is a concern with the car to put an offer "contingent" on a successful mechanic inspection. Mechanics are most useful when purchasing a higher dollar car out of warranty, when purchasing a collectors car, sports car, or exotic car, or when the buyer has no access to car-savvy helpers. While the decision to borrow more money than a seller could easily receive if they were to resell the vehicle, or to over-leverage themselves, is rarely a good one. It is essential for those in this buying scenario to consult a mechanic as repair costs would leave a buyer stranded and still owing more than a vehicle is worth.

Even with a mechanic's inspection, flaws and problems may be missed. In the same manner as car history reports, a mechanics inspection is simply a tool to bring in additional expertise where the buyer is lacking or to get a second opinion, with intent to assist in better understanding the car being purchased. Any time a car is being purchased, there is significant risk, and buyers should always assure they have money set aside for potential repair bills.

Buying Used Cars- How Much to Pay

Used car price calculations are significantly different than new car calculations. Determining the right price, whether buying a used car from an individual or from a dealer, begins in a similar manner. This is a challenge in the realm of used cars as there are few ways to truly establish what a seller will release a car for, nor how much a dealership paid for a car. This uncertainly opens up opportunities to get an excellent deal on a car purchase which can quickly lead to net-neutral car ownership or net-positive car ownership, but it just as easily can lead to overpaying for the same car.

The first thing a buyer must accept when looking for a used car is that they must be open to variables in what they are looking for, and if they find something they want they must be fully willing to walk away. Many dealers and owners will overvalue their own cars and demand a premium for them. As a buyer, it is important to recognize that unless the car is an extremely rare car or option package, in which a seller can clearly and openly "charge a premium", there will be similar cars available, and a buyer must evaluate a fair price for the car and refuse to stray far from the calculated price.

For buyers looking for great deals to establish net-neutral ownership and possibly net-positive ownership, the number they will pay will be much lower than someone just looking for a fair deal. This also means they will have to deal with a number of sellers turning down their offers, and they will effectively have to inquire and hypothesize into the "whys" with an aim of finding a car in which they can get at a lower price for one reason or another. These "Whys" can include situations such as a seller not knowing the value of the car, something wrong that needs to be repaired, or a seller urgent to sell.

Because the "right price" for a car will ultimately depend on the demands of the buyer, there is no simple calculation to nail a price down. There is an effective way to build baseline pricing. Once a baseline price is built, a buyer can then determine if cars they are evaluating for purchase are at price, overpriced, or underpriced. Depending on the situation however, overpriced cars can often be had for less than at-priced cars because often the seller will have a reduced number of people interested in the car, or a number of people who have left to say it is not worth it. This may make them more open to a lower offer. Just listed cars which are overpriced are typically not worth evaluating on the other hand.

To build a baseline, there is no more effective method than to research car listings. Keep in mind however that most people who list their cars are expecting someone to negotiate, and therefore the baseline shouldn't be set based on list prices, instead it should be built on expected sale pricing. For a novice, this can be difficult to evaluate, as they will often subconsciously baseline their pricing dependent on the numbers they see, as opposed to the actual sales price the cars would sell for.

Unlike with new cars, baselines vary with age, condition, location, colors, and options. This means that no two cars can be evaluated truly on par with another. For novices, one of the easiest ways to establish a baseline on what you believe is a "fair price", and then discount it by how much you anticipate the price will be negotiated. On cars under $1000, this is typically about $50-100. For cars $2500-$4500, this is about $250-500. On cars $5000 - $9000, its about $500-$800, and for cars over $10,000, it is usually $750-$1,250. There are always exceptions, but this offers a good baseline point. This does not mean this should be the actual offer, but rather it gives you an idea what the actual sale prices of the cars are likely to be.

Online guides offer an easier way to set a baseline, but typically buyers should assure they evaluate actual car availability as well. Online guides are very helpful establishing a baseline, but they are never completely accurate. Case in point, NadaGuides.com, which at the time of this publishing is widely regarded as one of the most accurate available guides, values a 2000 Corvette hardtop at between $7,200 and $10,225 depending on condition. It doesn't take long however on any listing service to discover this same car will be listed at $18,000 to $26,000 — and will sell for $16,000 or more. Many will sell for well over $22,000. A buyer who doesn't vet the online guides will spend their time frustrated as they cannot find sellers willing to enter what they perceive the value range is, while the sellers will know in most cases that their cars are worth more than double "book value". Like with most reference points, the online guides offer very valuable starting points and reference points, but smart buyers will not put too much weight on these car's book values when they see the markets dictating something much different.

Once a baseline for the car is established, then a buyer can evaluate any car compared to this baseline. If the condition is well above average, with lower miles, they will typically pay a premium over the baseline. If the condition is below average, or has high miles, they typically pay a discount under the baseline. The buyer then also weighs his or her own personal preferences. This means a buyer may choose to pay a little more for certain features, colors, or conveniences that increase the value to them as a buyer. At other times there are features, components, or concerns (such as waiting on a title or questionable history) that may make a specific buyer opt to discount the baseline for their personal purchasing. Typically this leads to a non-sale, but sometimes it can lead to a low-ball offer which is sometimes accepted. This can often lead to net-neutral or net positive purchases! Once a buyer evaluates the baseline, and adjusts the number based on their own demands and interests, they have their own accurate value for the car they are interested in. The buyer then determines the best negotiation tactic to meet or beat their valuation.

Brooks R Fiesinger

Buying a New Car- How Much to Pay

All the negotiation skills in the world can get a buyer only so far if they don't know how much they should be paying in the first place. To get a great deal on a car it is important to have as much information as possible, and this includes evaluating an accurate car price for comparison. Just because a buyer knows the "right price" for a car doesn't mean it's a great deal. Knowing the "right price" however, is the first step in assuring the deal a buyer is anticipating.

In order to determine how much a buyer should pay, the first step is to determine the dealer's true cost. The true cost is not the Manufacturer's Suggested Retail Price, or MSRP, nor is it the invoice pricing, as many dealers may like to lead consumers to believe. Instead, it is the invoice pricing, less the holdback and manufacturer's incentives. Invoice pricing is often available through dealerships, through online tools such as MSN autos and Edmunds.com, or through various building and research tools online and in print. Holdback is a set amount of money, or a percentage that a manufacturer repays to a dealership once the car is sold. In other words, the dealer pays the invoice price for the car, but once they sell it, they are repaid a certain percentage of that invoice or MSRP, typically 1-3% of MSRP. This is typically paid to a dealer quarterly. In addition, there are other types of similar repayments which also fall into this category. They include stock assistance, advertising credits, and other similar payments to the dealership. Incentives are a program where dealers are offered additional cash for the sales of particular cars. These are typically used to help move specific cars, trim levels, aid in specific markets, or to move out old stock as new models are ready to hit the floors. Incentives are not the same as rebates, and typically are not announced publicly, or advertised to consumers. A dealer is not required to disclose or pass on the incentives to a buyer. The first step is to evaluate the true cost the dealer must pay, which is this invoice price, minus holdback, minus incentives.

Once the true cost is determined, the next step is to accept that no business can operate at a loss or just break even. A dealership, like any other business, operates to make money. The business must make a fair profit. Profit is revenues (how much a buyer pays), minus expenses (how much the dealership must pay for the car delivered to the buyer). 3-4% is typically considered a fair profit, but buyers and circumstances may determine if it should be more or less. It is not worth anything to the dealership if they do not profit. It is important to note that in many cases, dealers may have to pay a finance cost or other charges, as well as operational charges to run the dealership. Another 1-2% should be added to cover these additional costs, ultimately leaving buyers with around 4-6% above actual dealer cost for a reasonable offer for most cars. It should be noted that for very high-dollar cars, this amount may be able to be dropped to 3-4%. While this is a good reasonable offer, this is just a beginning point when evaluating what a buyer ultimately will pay as there are additional rebates and charges that still must be factored in.

This reasonable offer value is then further discounted by any rebates. Rebates include any advertised deals or offers, often found on the dealer websites or manufacturer's websites, as well as many automotive informational websites. These often change month-by-month, and typically are not announced until close to mid-month. These rebates also typically expire at the end of the month. Other rebates are more permanent, including military rebates, college student and recent graduate rebates, and supplier pricing discounts. While many dealers may not want a buyer to realize this, these offers are rebated by the manufacturer, and therefore they do not affect the dealership's profits. Do note that some manufacturers have strict policies regarding further discounting some rebate programs, such as Friends and Family Discounts or Employee Pricing, but some dealerships have been known to forgo these policies, especially on a car that is not in high demand. Most rebates however do not include such policies.

Finally, the required charges such as the destination fee, taxes, and title are tacked on at the end. While it is important to include taxes in a buyer's personal calculation, when offering a final price to the dealer, taxes and title should not be included in the number. A buyer's final price minus taxes and title is the final dealer price. This leaves a buyer with three important numbers- A Reasonable Offer Price, which is the price to work the offer to, the Buyer's Final Price, which is the final price the buyer will pay to get the car off the floor and into their possession, and the Final Dealer Price, which is the final amount the Dealer will receive. These are the numbers that a buyer should have in hand ahead of time, and use when buying a car.

A common salesman tactic is to focus on monthly cost instead of final cost. A dealer can do a lot of things to get the "monthly" cost lower, which does not directly impact the ability of a buyer to get a good, or even fair deal. This includes extending terms over many years, which can as high as 120 months for specialty cars. Longer loan terms mean high interest rate costs, and payments on a car well after warranties have expired, leaving a car owner upside down on the car loan for the entire life of the car. Instead, buyers should balance the calculated Buyer's Final Price with what they can afford, either to buy outright or to properly finance. If a Buyer cannot truly afford the calculated Buyer's Final Price number, then it is time to move on to another, less expensive car without regard to any monthly offers or monthly costs stated by a salesman. If the buyer can afford the Buyer's Final Price, then getting a great deal is almost purely focused on the two remaining calculated numbers, the Reasonable Offer Price and the Final Dealer Price. Working to pay the Reasonable Offer Price is what will make a deal effective.

Once the Final Offer Price is agreed upon, then a buyer should look into financing rates and working to negotiate a lower rate. Only on special financing deals directly from the manufacturer's financing companies (such as 0% offers), do the dealership financing rates actually impact car cost. In the vast majority of these prime financing offers, it is a better deal for a buyer to actually finance through another company and take the bigger alternative rebates available for the cars.

This pricing model reflects the best pricing buyers are typically able to get for a standard, current model car. The absolute best values and deals in new car purchases on the other hand are cars that fall outside of this limitation. Past model cars, low demand cars, oddly-optioned cars, ordered cars that had a buyer fall through, or other unique variables are typically the only time a buyer can truly own a car net-neutral or net-positive when buying new. Most of the time these perspectives are effectively impacted in the rebates and Incentives calculated in this pricing model, yet dealers are occasionally willing to give up a portion of their 3-6% margin when they fear they will have to sit on a car a very long time.

The most effective new car buyers are individuals who are able to take advantage of the most effective rebates, incentives, and eager salesmen willing to take the lowest commission cut, such as new or inexperienced salesmen. This, coupled with the ability to find cars where the dealership needs to move a car, such as a one with diminishing value or continuing dealer financing costs, is effective. The best deals will be had in the situations when all three major parties, which includes the manufacturer , the dealership, and the salesman, are all more motivated to make a sale than a buyer is motivated to complete the sale. Good deals can be found when any one of those three components is extremely motivated. The best deals, such as net-positive and many net-neutral car buying experiences, are occasions in which all three parties are extremely motivated, driving the purchase price of the car down drastically.

It must be noted however that good salesmen, most dealerships, and none of the manufacturers will disclose when they are extremely motivated to sell. This means that a buyer must use intelligent speculation and research to determine these occasions. Beware of any situation in which a salesman or dealership acts overly eager to sell. Typically it is a strategy to move the sale through quickly. Most dealerships do occasionally sell a car at break-even or even a loss, but this is rare, and it takes a savvy buyer to take advantage of these rare opportunities when they arise.

While this pricing plan seems clear-cut, it can be challenging to determine the actual numbers necessary along the way. Web searches and data sheets can aid in showing holdback amounts and rebates, but incentives on the other hand can be difficult, especially since they often differ depending on the individual dealership! In lieu of extensive research breaking down each of these components, there are some great resources now available to help evaluate these numbers. One such tool is Edmunds True Market Value, or "TMV" available through Edmunds.com . Like other similar tools, these can help evaluate what the right price should be, but they limit themselves to a set of assumptions which mean they are not always accurate. When considering the time and research necessary to get all the necessary information however, the time commitment is not necessarily worth it for all buyers, which makes tools such as these an effective alternative.

New Car Discounts and Rebates Many People Don't Know Exist

There are often manufacturer rebates and discounts published at dealers, in the media, or on a manufacturer's website. While these are available for the general public to see and use, there are often many other discounts and rebates available to many eligible potential buyers of which the buyers are unaware. Most of the time, these rarely known discounts and rebates are from the financial arms of the manufacturers or from the manufacturers themselves. While some manufacturers have policies against further discounting, many smart buyers are able to get additional dealer discounts on cars a dealer is trying to move, or get other items of value such as additional trade-in allowance, significant accessory additions, or service agreements like free oil changes.

-Student and Graduate Discounts - Many manufacturers offer student and graduate deals, which can be a significant discount for

many buyers. Several manufacturers even offer a base supplier pricing plus additional rebates especially on cars which aren't moving as quickly as they hoped, and often offer a significant base rebate on high profile cars. ·Other manufacturers use the financial arms of their organization to offer special loan terms or the first month of a loan paid. Even an across the board cash rebate of $500 or $100 on top of whatever other deal a buyer works out is common. At the time of this publication, these student and graduate programs can sometimes offer as much as 26% off of the MSRP, which is a more significant discount than most other offers. Terms do depend on the manufacturer. Several are for current students, most seem to be for recent grads although some include individuals who have graduated over the previous several years. Several are also eligible for adults who are taking continuing education classes, making it worth looking into for many potential buyers.

-*Friends and Family Discounts* — While many buyers are aware that individuals who work for a dealership or manufacturer are eligible for discounts themselves, often they are unaware that these individuals are frequently permitted to share friends and family discounts with people they know. Some manufacturers offer a limited discount for unlimited numbers of friends and family, but may only allow two per year of a special class which are at a deeper discount. Asking around among friends and family, often a buyer is able to find someone who can share with them a Friends and Family discount. Some buyers have also found help through digital relationships, as some forum members will share friends and family discounts online.

-Supplier Pricing — According to the United States Department of Labor's Bureau of Labor Statistics (bls.gov), in February 2013, 3.65 million Americans worked for an automotive industry employer. Merging this with the US Census data for the number of households in the US, and accounting for some households having multiple members in the industry, as many as 3.2% of US households may be eligible for this discount. A buyer may not realize that a company they work for is actually eligible for supplier pricing. Some buyers find themselves part of a company that gets

supplier pricing simply because one single division of the company does business in the industry, making the entire corporation eligible. The corporation may have alternative agreements with a manufacturer that includes offering supplier pricing to members of its organization. It can be valuable to inquire about these discounts with all the employers in the family to determine if there are any supplier pricing opportunities available.

-*Groups, Clubs, and Affinity Groups* — Many buyers fail to realize that different groups from travel organizations to local and national car clubs often have discounts available for their members through certain manufacturers or dealerships. Several of them start at supplier pricing or even employee pricing on car purchases from certain makes. Often these are not strongly advertised, so a buyer may not be aware that the opportunities are available even in organizations of which they are already a member.

-*Referral Discounts*- Many car dealerships have "referrals", where they pay someone who refers a buyer to their dealership. While the referral typically goes to the person doing the referring, some dealerships offer a discount to both parties. In other cases however, asking a potential "referral" to split the referral bonus with you can shave a few bucks off the purchase price, and since the referrer is getting something for nothing already, they often won't hesitate to agree. If a buyer does not know personally of someone who has purchased from the corresponding dealership before, the buyer can jump on web forums to track down someone willing to split the referral in addition to offering authentic experience with the dealership. Typically however, a buyer may be surprised to find that with a limited number of dealerships in each geographic area, there is likely a personal contact who has shopped and purchased from this dealer before.

-In Market/Target Discounts — Often dealerships choose specific regions and market segments to target. A tell-tale sign to help a buyer discover if he or she is in the "target" group is when he or she begins to receive a variety of mailings from different dealers all at once. When a potential buyer is in a target segment, dealerships often have hidden

manufacturer discounts available as part of the campaign. These discounts can at times be more significant than many other discounts, and sometimes can be combined with other discounts. It is always helpful to ask or consider waiting for the buyer's next cycle to come up.

-Not really discounts, discounts- Other areas really affect the bottom line the same way a deal or discount does, and therefore deserve the time and attention buyers put into seeking out rebates and discounts. These can be as simple as getting a few percent lower interest rates on the car purchase, being able to buy a car without needing GAP insurance or getting true value-added features or services included. Ultimately it doesn't matter where the cost savings comes from, as long as it is there and can effectively affect the bottom line.

New and Used Car Dealer Add-Ons:

Determining if a buyer should purchase "add-ons" from a dealer, such as paint or interior treatment, extended warranties, or various other special offerings can be a difficult decision. The ultimate decision lies in the buyer's personal opinions regarding the additional "cost". For these items, the cost is purely a luxury, and it will never increase the ultimate value of the car for resale, and rarely do they pay off even as a convenience. From a financial perspective, even at discounted rates, they are not worth it. If the goal is to get the best deal and to own a car net-positive or net-neutral, the benefits tend not to pay out from a financial component. They are only worth it as a luxury convenience for those willing and able to pay for it.

A buyer determining if they should add on a 5 year total warranty to their new car discovered they were better off skipping it. The car included a 5 year drivetrain, and 3 year bumper-to-bumper warranty. The add-on warranty cost was $2230. The buyer was specifically concerned about if a replacement turbocharger would be included as a drivetrain. While ultimately, the drivetrain warranty appeared to cover the turbocharger, even if it did not the anticipated worst case scenario of the turbocharger going out still would not add up to the cost. After factoring in the cost with the added loan interest and Time Value of Money (TVM), the cost would have ended up being $2650 for the warranty, which is well over the cost of a replacement turbocharger installed. When pricing it out on a new-model car, remember the replacement part repair prices will decline over the first several years the car is on the market.

Car dealers often make a significant amount of money off of these deals, but buyers are better off turning them down. Sometimes a dealer will also have them "already included". They will often say it already has received paint treatment or interior treatment. Often after refusing to pay for them, the salesman will offer them at a "cheaper price", but without the warranty that comes with it. Eventually however, they will typically give up on the sale and won't charge a buyer for it, even if it has already been completed. As mentioned, if a buyer chooses to accept one of these add-ons, there is nothing inherently wrong with many of them as a luxury item, but they do not pay out in a financial manner for net-positive or net-neutral car ownership.

What to Look for in a Loan

Loans are often the last thing a buyer thinks about when they decide to buy a car. By the time the financing discussion emerges, the buyer has already fought their battle and determined if they are satisfied or not. The loan process is another area which is very important in minimizing the ultimate cost of car ownership. While it is best to shy away from loans when possible, they can be effective for many buyers as long as the buyer follows the *Rule of Maintaining Positive Equity* and is never "upside down" on the loan, owing more than their purchase is worth. When financing a car, it is important for buyers to come prepared prior to making the purchase decision, typically with another loan offer already in hand. In addition, it is important to assure that the loan conversation does not occur prior to the final price being agreed upon by the seller. It is a popular strategy for a salesperson to attempt to get the buyer to think "payments" and not "purchase price". The financing terms should always be a separate discussion after the final purchase price has been determined.

A popular sales tactic is to offer 0% loans on the purchase of a new car. However, 0% is typically not what it is cracked up to be. Often buyers are forced to give up other "rebates" in order to acquire the special 0% financing terms. While 0% may sound great on paper, a 1.75% rate with $2,000 in extra rebates is actually a much cheaper proposition for most car purchases. Even 6% interest rates may be cheaper if the rebate is higher, such as a $4,000-6,000 rebate, which can occur.

Coming to the dealership already prepared with loan terms is very important. Buyers should get their best rate from the buyer's bank or credit union before going to the dealer. If a buyer can join a credit union, often they have the best rates, although some bank loan programs do often offer excellent terms. Typically, dealerships will charge a higher loan rate than the company offering the loan is charging, and then will get the difference as what they call, "Dealer Reserve." This reserve is a payment back to the dealer for acquiring the loan. Unfortunately, this reserve adds another party as part of the loan cost, which frequently drives up the cost of the loan. While this may appear to be solely a negative, dealerships can often give up a portion of the reserve. This means that most of the time, if a buyer comes prepared with loan information, dealers are able to "beat" the loan offered from the buyer's bank or credit union. There are times where the dealership cannot always beat the offered price by the bank or credit union, in which case the car buyer can then use their personally acquired loan deal. Either way, getting a quote from the bank or credit union before visiting the dealership pays off significantly for the buyer.

It is also important for a buyer to never give up more leverage than necessary during the purchase. A buyer should let the dealership quote the loan, then alert them what the bank or credit union offered if it was lower. The dealership then has the opportunity to try use their agreements with lenders to attempt to beat the offer. If they cannot, then a buyer should go with their bank or credit union. If a buyer tells them about their loan prior to allowing the dealership to quote it, then the dealership will only try to beat the buyer's financing quote, which may not be the lowest possible rate.

It is important for buyers not to be too quick to consider certain loan terms as deal breakers. Regardless of rules of thumb and terminology, some things shouldn't be considered deal breakers in a loan.

Prepayment penalties are one example- While it may be a deal breaker with a $3500 prepayment penalty, the loans will often have a few hundred dollar penalty if a buyer pays it off in a short period, such as less than a year or within 6 months. If a buyer is confident he or she will keep a car that long, or if a significant rate reduction compensates for the prepayment penalty, then this term should not be a deal breaker.

To summarize, the loan process is an integral part of car buying for many buyers. It is important for buyers to complete the purchase agreement and then work to acquire the best financing deal, first by pricing out alternative financing options, and then negotiating them into the best financing deal available at the dealership. Buyers should beware of 0% financing offers, and should be sure to calculate out the real financing and interest charges over the life of the loan to maximize the value in their new car purchase.

The Rule of Maintaining Positive Equity

Many financial experts will say "Don't borrow money for a loan. It's not worth it". Some buyers on the other hand are quick to pick up a loan so they can get a better car. There is a more accurate way of weighing the financial expert's recommendation with a buyer's interest and desire to have a car they really want. To make sure the buyer is not getting into financial trouble when purchasing a car, the buyer should ensure they are following the "Rule of Maintaining Positive Equity".

Equity is the amount of money something is worth minus what is owed on it. In other words, if a buyer chooses a $25,000 car, and put $10,000 down on it, then they still owe $15,000, which is called the debt. If the used version of the car with say 10k miles on it would sell for $18,000, then this value is what we call the "Asset Value". A buyer can take the $18,000 "value", subtract the $15,000 they owe, and it leaves them with $3,000 remaining in asset value. This $3,000 is how much "Equity" a buyer has in the car. If this is a positive number, it is "Positive Equity". If this is a negative number, this is "Negative Equity". Negative equity often emerges when buyers don't put enough or any money down. In the above scenario, a buyer putting no money down would gain the $18,000 asset value, subtract the $25,000 debt, and emerge with a negative $7,000. This is "Negative Equity".

Car owners must be sure to estimate their car value effectively. The goal is to assure that at any time, the car can be sold for more than is owed on it, making it an "asset", and not a "debt" item to the owner. For this reason, car owners must be certain to make an accurate assessment of a vehicle's value as opposed to finding one car listing and presuming this is the value, or purely trusting a car guide or appraisal service. Instead, just like when creating a baseline for used car purchases, buyers should determine what the actual sales prices are from a variety of listings to generate their baseline, which in this case is the same as the "Asset value". Most owners will err on the side of a lower estimate, but the more accurate the assessment is, the more prepared the owner will be to make a good financial decision.

Car owners do not have to put money down in order to maintain positive equity. As an example, if a buyer were to buy a car from their aunt who can no longer drive, and she sells it to them for only $500 because she is trying to help them out, but it is worth $5,000, the buyer has $5,000 in positive equity, even without putting money down. In this scenario, the $500 purchase price is not a debt, but rather an upfront expense, and the value of the asset is $5,000. $5,000 minus $0 in debt is $5,000. The same can be true of buying cars even on the market. If a special circumstance car allows someone to purchase a Lexus for $14,000, and the true market value is closer to $15,000, then without even putting a penny down, the $14,000 in debt is less than the $15,000 asset value, retaining positive equity.

The Rule of Maintaining Positive Equity simply means: Don't ever buy a car unless positive equity can be maintained. If a buyer cannot put enough money down, or doesn't have a big enough trade in, or cannot get the car they want for a low enough price to maintain positive equity, then this buyer cannot afford the car, and should not be purchasing it.

Total Cumulative Positive Equity

Total Cumulative Positive Equity, or TCPE is an advanced method beyond simply "Maintaining Positive Equity." This is more challenging, but can allow a buyer to be financially safe, in addition to assuring their car purchase is a fair investment at net-neutral or net-positive. This requires the buyer to effectively combine the car selection, price, financing, maintenance and resale in an effective proportion.

TCPE is truly "Getting a great deal." It is not simply "maintaining positive equity," but rather making sure throughout the entire ownership process of the car, a buyer maintains Total Cumulative Positive Equity. In other words, the car is always worth more than is owed AND worth more than a buyer has invested in it combined, including down payments, financing costs, repair costs, purchase price, and typically even registration fees and taxes. The term "Flipping Houses" has become commonplace, and some individuals have begun using the term "Flipping cars", which means buying cars under value, typically which need work, fixing them, and reselling them. Flipping cars as a profit generation method works, but requires extensive expertise. A limited form of flipping cars where the buyer works to assure they purchase at bottom dollar, maintain the cars effectively, monitor the market during car ownership, and resell effectively can offer TCPE without having to understand how to work on cars or have inside access to resources not readily available. For the average person, TCPE can be a rewarding opportunity to essentially erase the typically high cost of car ownership, and turning cars away from a pricey "expense", into an investment tool, changing the way owners view their car ownership.

Brooks R Fiesinger

Extreme Savings Opportunities Through Separable Value-Add Items

The ultimate cost of a car has a lot to do with the amount of time and effort a buyer wants to spend. Getting a great deal involves a lot of research, flexibility, and legwork. The opportunity to get an amazing deal may actually involve a deal that isn't quite so impressive up front, but in the big picture really adds up.

One area this is very evident is through a concept called Separable Value-Add Items, or SVAI for short. SVAIs are anything included in a purchase up front which can actually be separated from the car without diminishing the value of the car significantly. While free oil changes and recommended service is included in many new car deals, those looking for extreme savings are going to find that the real SVAIs go well beyond this.

SVAIs come in many shapes and sizes, and the more knowledgeable a buyer is about a car, the better opportunity they have to spot them. Most SVAIs go unnoticed by potential buyers and sellers, or are items which don't influence the actual purchase price of a car, and this is where the true opportunity comes into play. SVAIs are typically items included in a sale which can easily be separated and resold for significant amounts of money, effectively lowering the price of the car- If a buyer spends $16,000 on a car which comes with $4,000 in SVAIs, this $16,000 initial cost minus the $4,000 leaves the buyer giving up $12,000 for the car. In this case, $12,000 may be a great deal on a car when $16,000 was only an OK deal.

A perfect SVAI opportunity came to the author when he purchased a lightly used, current model BMW from someone trying to unload it quickly so they could purchase another car. He paid the approximate trade-in-value for the car, which makes it a good deal to begin with, but it didn't end there. The car came with a separate set of BMW wheels and Blizzak Winter tires in great shape. Checking Craigslist and Ebay, the author saw this set was going for about $1000-1200. He was able to sell the set for just over $1000 without even having to take anything off the car! This car also had a BMW performance Exhaust. While "aftermarket" exhausts often are worth little to nothing, brand name performance exhausts often are. In this case, the performance exhaust had a retail value of about $1250. Most buyers wouldn't pay more for this exhaust, meaning it could be removed without detracting from the value of the car. The author found a local enthusiast interested in trading their stock exhaust plus $1000 for the performance exhaust, making it beneficial to both parties. Just those two SVAIs alone offered a quick and easy $2100, which effectively reduced the "cost" for the car below auction value. It can now be driven for a significant period of time with regular maintenance, and then still sell for the same price (or better) than what was paid initially!

There were other SVAIs available on this car that would have been easy to sell, and many others which would have been a little more difficult, but still could have been possible depending on how aggressive the buyer wanted to be. The 18" sport wheels with run flat tires could have been sold for more than the winter wheels, and the winter wheels could have been installed on the BMW netting a higher SVAI price. The car also included an extra set of wheel bearings and LED halo lights which could have easily been sold. Other things which are more common are also SVAIs.

For example, the car also had its original manual, and original manuals depending on the make can often sell for $50-100! Premium parts such as shifter knobs, GPS Map DVDs, and other similar parts could have also netted even more.

On different types of cars, there are many other types of SVAIs. If a truck is purchased, the buyer may be able to sell Brake controllers and Hitches which could net $500 or more. Others include removable bed liners, tonneau covers and bed caps. A convertible or small SUV may come with a soft top and a hard top- the hard top could be sold for $1000. On cars, Specialty wheels can be sold and replaced with stock wheels. Rear sun screens, hatch dividers, Step bars, cosmetic trim, high end stereos, and radar detectors are all potential SVAIs that could net significant amounts of additional cash post-purchase.

Another unique area for SVAIs, especially among those who "flip cars", are hidden as "upgrades" in some of the indispensible, typical parts such as headlights, taillights, and body panels, intakes, and even engine and drive train components. This can be done by replacing them with aftermarket parts. Typically looked at as an "expense" for a car owner which they partake in for performance gain or cosmetic interest, often these are hidden SVAI opportunities! The cheapest used Maserati Coupe front bumper cover on eBay is $1500 at the time of this publication. However, an aftermarket bumper, which many people buy to give them an improved look, can be purchased for $260. Doing the same with the rear bumper and side skirts, $4000 could be extracted from the car without lowering its sales value. This isn't limited to high end luxury Italian cars. New model Ram headlights are running $550, while aftermarket headlights are available for $159, potentially netting $390, while the taillights could net another $350. Stock navigation systems can often be replaced by aftermarket units, resold for more than the aftermarket unit cost. These types of SVAIs are more frequently available than many realize, disguised as "upgrades" which can turn into more money than the upgrade costs.

Often buyers fail to pay attention to SVAIs, yet these are often areas where the best deals can be found. This is because sellers often just "include everything", yet these inclusions often aren't reflected as part of the pricing negotiations. While some SVAIs may not be worth the time and effort, some SVAIs are extremely straight forward and generate additional cash which enhances the buyer's financial position.

Section 2:

Leasing a Car

Leasing a Car

Everything has a "cost". For those who don't want to negotiate, or deal with the hassles of research or reselling their cars, the best option is often to lease a car. While this costs a premium compared to well researched and negotiated purchasing behavior, it simplifies the process drastically. It prevents the need for any non-warranty repair work, simplifies the "sales" and repurchase process, and is not a bad way to acquire transportation for those busy professionals who can afford this "premium".

While most people seem determined to get a "great deal" when they purchase a car, the cost in time to make sure that happens truly isn't worth it for everyone. Hours of research, negotiation, and potential calculations may not be worth the time it takes. Other buyers may be interested in leasing a car in order to use it as a business expense, or for other personal reasons. Just because a buyer chooses to get a lease, doesn't mean their position can't be improved.

There are still strategies, including negotiation, to improve the leasing experience for the buyer.

Negotiating a Lease:

Contrary to the belief of some, leases are negotiable just as car purchases are. When leasing a car, the sale company is essentially "selling" it to a buyer and pre-contracting a buy-back after several years. While this is certainly not the terminology used in leasing, from the functional perspective, this is essentially the basics behind the lease process. The selling company is looking to maximize the value they can get from the initial lease and then the resale of the vehicle. In other words, they want to maximize the value of both sales (initial and secondary), while minimizing their costs on both perspectives.

What this means to a buyer is that a car that will be worth more at the end of the lease, will have more value to the selling company. This means that the first step in getting a good lease deal is to choose the right car to lease. By purchasing a car with a higher resale value, a potential buyer is improving the position for the selling company, and therefore opening up more room for negotiations. To evaluate the future price, a buyer can evaluate a few factors. This includes the desirability of the make and model, as well as how the model fits into the larger car market. Current generation cars, which are cars near-identical to the newest body style and features, for example will be worth more than past-generation cars. Buying a car and returning it as part of the lease while it is still the "current generation" will mean it retains more value than a car which had crossed generations. A good way to evaluate the "end of lease value", which is known as its "Residual Value" in the industry, is to use both independent research and intelligent speculation, as well as Residual Guides which are available both online and through the "Automotive Lease Guide" available from alg.com. This guide is often also available in local libraries, and the Residual Guides are updated monthly. In the vast majority of situations, buyers want to find a car with a higher residual value. The "cost" is the difference between the new car value and the residual value, so a higher residual value in a lease lowers the ultimate "cost".

There are exceptions to looking for high residuals. One example includes using a leased car for legitimate business purposes, and then choosing to purchase the car afterwards for personal use. A low residual will leave a higher burden on the business during the lease period, but a lower burden on the individual when the lease is up.

Once the right cars are found, just like in buying a car new, buyers should investigate special manufacturer lease deals. When a manufacturer is extensively motivated to move specific cars, they often offer lease deals which are below their typical lease offers.

Once the car is identified, the buyer should negotiate the value of a car just as if they were buying the car. The "cost" to the buyer is the difference between the new car price and the residual price, plus interest and fees. By lowering the new car price, they cut the gap, lowering their ultimate cost. Many experts believe, as when discussing financing terms, choosing not to discuss leasing until a sale price is agreed upon can be effective. This sale price will be called the capitalized cost when used in a lease. On top of this capitalized cost, there will also be an acquisition fee from the bank, which should be anticipated in advance, as well as a disposition fee when the car is returned. Combined, these are almost always under $1000.

In leasing cars, the "interest" is actually called a "Money Factor". The Money Factor is the interest being paid to the dealership/bank for letting a leasing individual use the car. It compensates the dealership or bank for the risk of a leasee not paying, as well as the opportunity cost of the money, using it for the leasee as opposed to other opportunities. By leasing the car, the dealership or bank is unable to use the money in other ways such as lending it to others or purchasing other goods. The Money Factor is calculated by evaluating the interest rate divided by the number 2400. In other words, a money factor of .0025 is the equivalency of 6% Annual Percentage Rate Interest.

When discussing the specific lease, an interested individual should make sure the lease fits his or her anticipated usage. Leases can often be drawn up with 10,000 to 15,000 mile per year mileage allowances. Since overages can be incredibly costly, buyers should assure the mileage allowance fits into their expected use, and that the lease is drawn up accordingly. Contract length is another significant area where a buyer must ensure it fits his or her needs. Leases can range from 24 months to six years, and sometimes during negotiations, these time periods can be adjusted longer as hidden concessions. Be sure to note and monitor the lease terms throughout the negotiation process. Other contract specifics will include special fees, such as the acquisition fee, disposition fee, and purchase option fees, and while these should be anticipated, if any of them seem uncomfortably large, it is worth investigating further or walking away. Leases may also potentially hide additional costs such as taxes, license, and required GAP Insurance. A smart buyer should ask (and check the contract) regarding what potential expenses will be involved.

Another area to consider is Trade-In Values. Buyers can trade in a car (or sometimes more than one car) on the lease of a car, which is deducted from the capitalized cost similar to a new car purchase. The Trade-In values can be negotiated in the same manner for lease car as they can for a new car purchase, and negotiating a higher trade-in value can often have a major impact on the ultimate lease cost.

Leasing can be a car acquisition method which works well for many buyers. It is important for these leasees to consider all the components of a lease, and work to assure they are setting up the lease in a manner to minimize their costs while maximizing the benefit they get through the car acquisition.

Section 3:

Owning a Car

Brooks R Fiesinger

Owning a Car

An award winning businessman once stated, "Always run your business like it's for sale". To get the best price for a car, sellers have to maintain the same mentality. Always own your car as if it is always for sale. It is essential to keep the car in great running condition. Proper maintenance and upkeep are important. Repair problems as they emerge, and always pay attention to the car and the market with eyes and ears open.

A seller may not notice how often someone says "I wish I could find a car like yours" or "When are you going to sell it?" Frequently these are said in jest, but all too often there is a legitimate interest behind those words. Make a mental note of who said it, so that when selling the car the seller can reach out to these people. It is also important to be prepared to sell it when it has peak value. By paying attention to market conditions and car values, a car owner can be sure to sell their car while it still holds a high value, which is an integral component of net-neutral and net-positive car ownership.

The peak value depends on the car. Collector and Performance Cars like a Corvette often see a value spike when a new model is introduced, while luxury cars will often see its value plummet when a new model is introduced. It appears that Collector/Performance cars are more timeless in design, with a large legion of followers. When potential buyers are inspired by the new models that emerge, they quickly realize they are out of their price range, and their interest in older versions of the car which they can afford grows, leading to higher demand for the older versions. Luxury cars on the other hand see values drop as soon as a new version hits the market. It appears as if there is a lot of consumer value in having the current style for lifestyle and fashion purposes. In addition, Luxury car designs tend to be less timeless, leading older versions to quickly fall out of favor in preferred design elements in ways not seen in the performance and collector car markets. Differentiating marks such as special headlight designs, grilles, and marks that set the model apart when new, now begin to stand out as giant flags pointing out the seasoned elements of the aging cars. This often makes for a great time to buy a luxury car if the fashion and lifestyle components are less valuable to a buyer, as several year old low-mileage luxury cars may be available at a tiny fraction of their initial pricing.

By monitoring the markets and maintaining their car's condition, an owner can sell their car and buy a new one when it is most financially sound. This tends to effectively preserve the car owner's financial interests.

Playing the Game of Generations

There are two sides to every decision, and the most successful decisions are based on weighing them both. Due to the amount of information available and processed during the car buying process, human nature often leads to overvaluing tidbits of information which can lead buyers to make irrational buying decisions. One area this is valid is in purchasing early-model year cars as opposed to late model cars.

Many new car buyers refuse to purchase the first model year of a new car because their rationale is that the first year is filled with bugs and problems which are ironed out in later years. They believe that by waiting a more reliable car will be available. While this argument seems logical for new cars, it has questionable value at best and little to no value for used cars. When buying a New Car, very few cars are "completely new". Even cars sold as "completely new" are modified versions of other cars. The brand new never before seen 2014 Chevrolet SS was based on the Holden Commodore previously available in Australia, which utilizes the same Zeta platform used in the Chevrolet Camaro. The same car also uses a tried and true engine platform pulled from the Corvettes. Many new engines that emerge today are either fine-tuned versions of prior motors, or in the case of new motors, are often the same motors used even by other makes. New Transmissions are often either based on past transmissions or are the same transmission used on other makes also. The Chrysler Crossfire, which launched in 2003 used the same engine and transmission as well as around 80% total of the parts and components from the Mercedes SLK 320, which came out in 2001, meaning most of the mechanics were already "tried and true". The 2001 SLK wasn't an "all new" car either, and was based on the SLK 230 which emerged back in 1996, and used the same 3.2 liter motor from a variety of Mercedes cars since 1998.

In short, modern cars are already a mix of parts already on the market from different companies in different countries. Innovations are almost always incremental in the automotive industry, with minor updates to a component here or there to generate more power or improved features. Never does a new car come out with all new parts and components, and therefore even a new model year car is mostly tried and true.

There is one other major innovation which has changed this thought process, and that is computerized testing. Computerized testing has allowed manufacturers of cars to do such in depth testing of any new parts so when cars hit the market, the confidence level on a newly designed part is much higher.

While there still may be an occasional recall, it often doesn't come for several years, and when it does, it is typically a minor issue easily repaired by the manufacturer. Rarely is it a design flaw without an easy solution.

Even on used cars any potential flaw with an early model car will be known, and any recalls should be addressed and repaired, with rare exceptions. Most concerns are vastly overplayed. On those exceptions however, it isn't the fact that it's a new model year that is the issue, it's that there are specific model years that are issues. These issues can emerge in early or later years. According to MSN Autos[4], who gathers their information from AIS (Auto Information Services), a reliable source of repair statistics, 2006, the first year of the remodeled 3-series BMW had a "5 out of 5" reliability rating, as did 2007- however, the same body style in 2008 was plagued with "significant problems" receiving only a 4 out of 5 overall. In this case, the early years many buyers shy away from due to fear of potential manufacturing concerns, were more reliable than the later years of the same body style. Other cars while retaining the same "body style" receive significant changes to engines or other major components, often for reasons unrelated to reliability such as cost or horsepower.

In both cases, whether a buyer purchases a car new or buys it used, once the buyer chooses to resell the car, the car falls into only one category, "Used". When sold as used, body style is much more important than the manufacturing year, and therefore should be the focal point of evaluating potential resale. Using a random mix of makes and models and using this with information found from Kelley Blue Book, a buying guide and pricing service used frequently in the industry, the difference in price between the oldest car in a generation to the newest car in the prior generation is six times higher than the difference between yearly generations alone. In other words, the body style is six times more important than the actual year the car was produced. This means that the first year of a new body style will depreciate less per year than any other year of the car style, and buying first year body styles will tend to preserve its value better than other years in the body style.

This also goes to show that when the body style changes, the value of the car will drop drastically. Maximum value can be derived from a car sold during its current body style even if it is a few years old, as opposed to a car which is newer in age, but has an older body style. The value drops off in steps, and so even after a body style change, the value of a car will be closer to other cars of the same body style than they are of other cars closer in year. For example, a 1997 Corvette is valued closer to a 1998 Corvette, while a 1996 Corvette is worth only a fraction of the 1997 as it is a different body style. The same is said about BMWs and Pontiacs, and most everything in between. This also means that buying early model cars will preserve their value better even if it isn't the most current body style.

The benefit of buying the first year or two of a new body style outweighs the risks in modern automotive markets, and becomes an effective way to preserve a car's value. For this reason, early model year cars for each body style are most preferred when buying and selling, contrary to popular belief, and especially important for buyers looking for net-neutral or net-positive car ownership.

Exceptions and Specialty Cars

There really are few hard set rules that every car buyer must follow. Depending on the type of situation, the type of year, the type of buyer, and the type of seller, different strategies and different considerations emerge. While the ultimate variations are endless, there are a few specific specialty cars which find themselves often as the exception and not as the rule.

For high performance cars such as the Chevrolet Corvette, values of old model years can shoot up briefly when a new model emerges. This is contrary to other cars such as luxury cars, coupes, and sedans where prior generations drastically drop in value the minute a new generation emerges. This is because of the high desirability, yet high cost, of these new cars. When a new high performance car comes out such as the C7 Corvette, they emerge with an extreme amount of emotion and fanfare. Enthusiasts, who are unable to afford the high priced car, turn to what they can afford, and spike the demand for the older alternatives temporarily driving up their prices.

One other type of car that preserves its value in abnormal fashion are high end cars and popular cars which have a strong following. Examples include the Plymouth Prowler and the Pontiac G8 (namely the high performance GXP, and the GT trims to a lesser degree). When Pontiac closed its doors in 2010, the popular 4 door performance Sedan, the G8 was discontinued alongside it. Pontiac, while not strong enough for General Motors to keep open as part of its portfolio during the recession occurring at the time, had a strong following of loyal fans, and the G8 ended up being one of the most powerful cars ever produced by Pontiac. This has allowed these performance cars to preserve their value well after production ended, and four years after they were discontinued, used GXP trims with average mileage are selling for only 14% less than a buyer would pay for one new in 2009. Popular collectable cars which are being discontinued often become great targets for net-neutral and net-positive car purchases.

There may be other exceptions as well, but any time there is an "exception", there is a strong reason behind it. The exception must follow basic business principles of creating tighter supply or higher demand. These principles can also help potential buyers determine when the best time is to "own" a car. A seller can maximize the value of their cars, and when analyzed and timed properly, sellers can enjoy high profile, fun and exciting cars without losing a lot of money to do so.

Maintaining Value and Staying Safe

Buying and Selling may be the focus points of saving money and preventing a car owner from losing money on their car ownership, but the car's maintenance is important as well. Being smart about maintenance can assure a car owner can get top dollar for their car when they sell it, and prevent a car owner from having to spend significant money on major car problems in the process.

Even if a car is going to be owned for only a short time, car maintenance will help prevent a major disaster costing the owner a large amount. Maintenance that should be completed for virtually every gasoline powered car on the market include oil changes and air filters. Cars owned for any significant length of time and driven a number of miles may also need brake fluid, transfer case fluid, transmission fluid, differential fluid, power steering fluid, fuel filters, coolant, drive belts, spark plugs, joint lubrication, hoses, water pumps, oxygen sensors, cabin filters, and timing belts. Be sure to inspect timing belts and other belts regularly, as a failed timing belt can often lead to an entire engine replacement on interference-style engines. Every car is slightly different so specific car manuals should always be referenced when determining the best way to care for a car. It is important for buyers to beware of cars which have "lifetime" fluids with no maintenance plan. When a manufacturer refers to "lifetime" fluids, they typically mean the lifetime of the initial buyer, not the lifetime of the car. This means that owning the car past 100,000 miles or longer than an average new car purchase would necessitate fluid changes which may not be dictated in the manual. These can include, but are not limited to transmission fluid, differential oil, and transfer case fluid.

With repair shop times approaching $100 per hour[2] or more in many jurisdictions, the number of do-it-yourselfers (DIYs) in the automotive industry is astounding, and has facilitated the growth of companies such as AutoZone, Pep-Boys, Napa, O'Reillys, and Advance Automotive, as well as significant automotive sections of stores such as

Walmart, Meijers, and Target. There are plenty of companies providing parts, and often an owner doesn't need to be a mechanic to do many repair and maintenance items on their own. Car-specific forums and repair guides available at many retailers can aid even a novice DIY, allowing them to maintain their own cars and repair issues for a fraction of the cost of repair shops or dealerships. On a 2001 Mercedes SLK for example, fixing a non-working convertible top was quoted at thousands of dollars from the dealer, yet a $17 gasket kit available by members of a forum was able to easily repair the top in less than a day, saving the owner thousands of dollars. Tricks and kits such as this are readily available for a variety of makes and models on these car-specific forum websites.

By using low-cost retailers, often a car owner can acquire maintenance parts and repair parts at a fraction of dealership rates, but only when the parts are of comparable quality. Especially when owning a higher performance car, a luxury car, or one with something unique about it, not all "fluids" or "parts" may be truly comparable and suitable for usage, even if the seller so claims. In addition to generic parts which can often be found at these retailers, more specific parts can often be acquired at extremely low costs from places such as eBay, Craigslist, and local junk yards. Using non-oem (Original Equipment Manufacturer) parts when appropriate can also save significant money, as long as a quality part is still used. Even body panels such as bumpers and side skirts as well as lights are often available in an alternative format, often sold as an "upgrade", which may be significantly cheaper than an OEM replacement part.

Proper maintenance is essential for any car ownership. If a buyer is not interested in doing it themselves, using local shops and even dealerships can still be an affordable method to preserve the car's condition, and does not have to be a deal breaker.

Finding a Shop

Anyone who owns a car should do their due diligence in finding a repair shop before they need repairs done. Even those who are extremely knowledgeable, and intend to do their own work should still do their due diligence in finding a shop. Everyone occasionally needs help, doesn't have the time, skill, or tool to perform a certain task, or ends up with unexpected emergencies.

It is best to seek out a shop and over time build a relationship with them. When they know a car owner will be bringing them repeat business, and they get to know the owner and their cars, repairs can be cheaper and quicker to diagnose. They may offer the owner significant benefits such as occasional discounts, doing extra little things without charging for them, or at a minimum making sure everything is completed to an owner's complete satisfaction. Buyers often can also save money by making sure only the repairs needed are completed.

Most people find a good shop by asking acquaintances where they take their cars. If a prospective customer is unsure who they should ask, they can keep their eyes open for someone they know, or a relative of someone they know, who tends to work on cars or is knowledgeable about cars. It is important for the referral to come from someone knowledgeable about cars, as many people will recommend wherever they go themselves simply to validate their own decisions, regardless of the shop's quality. Other places to look include car-enthusiast forums, and local car enthusiast groups. Web-based ratings and reviews have limited reliability, as many of them are managed by the companies themselves.

It is important not to let the "name" of the repair shop influence a car owner's repair shop decisions. Whether it is a chain, a dealership, or a mom-and-pop shop, almost every one is locally owned and operated. Simply because a customer has a good experience at one chain location does not mean another location with a different owner will be as good. The same is true with bad experiences. The name itself would not help distinguish the shop quality.

Once a customer has selected a shop, they may choose to go with a "dry run" by bringing the car by for something simple such as an oil change, just to see how the shop operates. Most well run shops will have a variety of mechanics, from younger inexperienced mechanics who will do basic jobs, to experienced mechanics who work on the most challenging projects and work with the most important cars. In doing due diligence, a customer should take an active role in the work being performed. Watch what they are doing through the window, ask questions before hand, and when it is all done, tip the mechanic who worked on your car a few dollars. The due diligence isn't simply so a customer can vet the repair shop, rather it's also an opportunity for the shop to see that the customer is worth keeping happy and treating right.

If a customer is not pleased with their experience, or if something does not seem right about the shop or the way it is run, this is the time to go ahead and make it a one-visit shop. An owner should take their car elsewhere, as there are plenty of high quality shops available to service a customer's needs.

Two special areas of concern when working with a shop is to monitor how much time the shop charges for the work performed, and how much they charge for parts. For parts, most shops have differing rates of "upcharge". Many shops charge double their cost on a part, while others upcharge by 50%. Many others upcharge based on a sliding scale depending on the cost of the parts in question. While shops should be expected to do so to make money, these numbers are rarely disclosed to customers. Those visiting the shops should monitor these charges as they select their preferred shop.

The second concern is shop time. Contrary to what may seem like "common sense," one hour of shop time does not equal one hour of time worked. Shops utilize software packages and books to determine what is the "shop time" for each piece of work performed. This allows them to offer accurate quotes and allocation of projects. All shops do this to some extent, and often they complete the work faster with special tools or multiple service members, which all have their associated costs. However, different books and software packages may offer significantly different amounts of time for each repair, which may add up. More significantly, some shops add in their own additional mark-up time for different procedures. This means that while one shop may have a higher per-hour repair cost, the repair bills may ultimately be significantly cheaper. For a battery replacement in a 2006 BMW 330i as an example, one software package dictates 1.5 hours of shop time while another shop dictates 30 minutes of shop time. Even though the prior shop lists their price at $97 per hour and the latter quotes $114, the latter shop ultimately saves the owner over 60%.

Brooks R Fiesinger

Section 4:

Selling a Car

Determining Trade-In or Private Party Sale

As part of the purchasing a car, buyers must also determine if they will be trading in an old vehicle. Dealer Trade Ins are an area that tend to get a bad rap, often unnecessarily. A common misconception is that people can get a "lot more money" if they sell it to a private party as opposed to trading it in. While frequently a seller can get "more money", it is not enough to generate a hard and fast rule. Often a trade in is both easier and more financially sound than a private party sale, even if it does not appear so on the surface.

To understand why trading in is often a good alternative, sellers need to consider all the costs involved. It is fairly universal that people believe "their" things are worth more than "someone else's", and therefore they over-value what they own. This leads people to "believe" they will sell their car for much more than they will. These sellers often look at websites such as Ebay, Craigslist, and Autotrader and value their cars at what others are listing them at- or even higher in many cases, as they believe theirs is in "better" condition. They forget to compensate for the fact that buyers rarely pay listing prices, and often negotiate to a significantly lower price. Sellers need to recognize that the actual selling price is typically significantly below the list price.

Sellers also need to realize what they are leaving on the table when they choose to sell to a private party. In many municipalities, when purchasing a new car, buyers don't have to pay the sales tax on the value of their trade in. On a $25,000 trade in, this can often be $2000 or more saved in taxes alone. This means that a $25,000 trade in offer may be about the same ultimate "value" as a $30,000 private party listing, as the Trade In offer will save $2,000 in taxes, and the Private Party listing may see a $3,000 drop via offers and negotiations. It is also important for a seller to factor in selling costs, such as holding the car on insurance longer, gas for test drives, and listing fees for sales avenues such as Ebay and AutoTrader.

Another thing to consider, especially with high dollar cars, is how easy they are to sell. Years ago, it was nearly impossible for a private buyer to get a car loan to buy from a private seller. In recent years however, this has shifted, and private buyers are able to get loans for private sales. It often requires a time consuming process that could add complications to scheduling a sale. Cars under $10,000 are often sold for cash amounts, but those higher priced cars depend on someone being able to get a private party loan. This means it can take a long time to find a buyer who can actually pay cash or can arrange financing. If a seller still owes on a car, many buyers will be hesitant to complete the purchase as well. Lenders often take several weeks before the title is sent to the buyer, which means the buyer is forced to trust the seller with their payment before the title can be transferred. It also prevents a buyer from being able to register the new car for several weeks, which can often be a deal-breaker for someone who needs transportation.

As a seller, it's also imperative to determine if it is worth the time investment, as it can be significant. Time to list a car, time to be home to offer test drives, time to answer phone calls and respond to emails, and even time to take photos of the car all add up and may not be worth the efforts. Work schedules or busy weekends can make it difficult to line up meetings with potential buyers, and time lost from other activities such as work or family may have emotional or actual cash costs as well.

Lastly, if a seller chooses to sell as a private party, they must determine if they will sell it before buying a new car, or after buying a new car. Before buying a new car, they must consider the loss of leverage during the buying process, and a rushed purchase decision. Both tend to lead to higher prices being spent on the car being purchased. These added costs can often make private party sales ultimately more expensive than trading the car in! If a seller chooses to wait until after buying the new car, they need to have enough cash available to do so. This is a deal-breaker for many, as is having to maintain insurance on multiple cars during the sales process, and having to house and maintain both cars until the old car has been sold.

When considering all of these additional "costs" to private party sales, sellers often determine that trading in their car is actually an intelligent move that may even save them money. Considering all factors, they may determine a private party sale is better, especially for low-dollar cars.

Specifics of Selling a Car

In order to enjoy cars without losing a significant sum of money, car owners must pay as much attention to selling their cars as they do buying them. Getting an extra thousand dollars when selling is just as beneficial as getting an extra thousand dollars off when buying, yet many sellers tend to put much less attention into selling. In order to achieve net-neutral and net-positive car ownership, good selling is essential.

Selling cars is essentially the inverse of buying a car, and for this reason, the best way to be an effective seller is to know and understand how buyers purchase cars. When it is the best time to buy, it's the worst time to sell, and when it's a bad time to buy, it becomes a good time to sell. The most important principle of selling a car is simply patience. Car owners tend to sell low because they are nervous another seller won't come around, or they cut their prices because they see other sellers drastically cutting their prices during a temporary influx of cars on the market. For a seller, patience, strategy, and planning can go a long way.

Sellers should look at car-sales as a lengthy proposition. While it is very possible to sell a car in a few days at a fair price, a seller should be prepared for, and not be concerned if several weeks or months pass without selling the car. Sellers have to be careful they don't fall into the numerous traps that savvy buyers can walk them into, or the short term market pitfalls that tend to emerge.

The basics of selling are to sell when demand is high and the supply is low, listing the price effectively, and then attempting to maintain maximum leverage during the negotiations. In the private party realm of car sales, demand can fluctuate on the slightest of changes, from a new car announcement, to the outside temperature, or even to the time of the month. On the other side of the same token, as sellers attempt to get best price for their product, they often create pockets of significant supply which can also drive price down, such as 2-seater roadsters at the onset of summer and 4x4 trucks at the onset of winter. Leverage can be maximized by assuring there is no rush to sell, assuring the car is in the "right" condition for the market, and effectively navigating buyers to reduce their leverage in the buying process.

When a seller researches their car and the market, and accurately analyzes the proper pricing for a car, it becomes much easier to resist succumbing to low offers, short-term demand dips and temporary supply peaks.

When to Sell

Unlike buying, when selling a car there isn't much opportunity to fine tune the car being sold dependent on current market conditions. It does help however to monitor the lifecycles of the car being sold. Typically it helps to sell before a new body style emerges on the market, which is often 5-6 years after introduction of a new style. As soon as a new body style emerges, the costs of all previous generations drop in real market value drastically. The time of year is important as buying times for vehicles vary with the seasons, new car launches, and financial situations. It is important for sellers to anticipate game theory as well, hitting the market before most sellers list their vehicles for the seasonal demand, and if the car is unsold by the time prices drop, it is best to simply wait a few weeks for the supply to begin to dry up again.

Where to Sell

There are endless possibilities in determining where to sell a car, from online forums to online listings and auctions, to dealerships, magazines, newspapers, and an owner's front lawn. The best places to sell are largely dependent on the type of car being sold, the timeline of the seller, and the location of the seller.

Unfortunately, most sellers do not have an opportunity to decide what geographical region best suits their vehicle. Many regions pay premiums for certain types of cars, while other regions pay a discount for the same cars. Some sellers find themselves between two geographic regions, travel for work, or have a vacation property, and can choose to list in the region best suited for their vehicle type. For those sellers who do have this opportunity to sell between multiple locations, baseline price evaluations can be analyzed to maximize profit potential. For most sellers however, the decision is not what town, city, or state to sell in, but rather what sales method to pursue.

For cars which benefit from a broad range distribution, or where local buyers are limited, such as for a classic car, collectors car, specialty car, or supercar, a sales avenue that reaches out to a broader group of buyers is often effective. To quickly sell one of these cars, one of the most effective and cost effective methods is eBay. While eBay does charge a large chunk sum when the car is sold, they do not charge the seller until a sale is made. The more significant negative of selling on eBay is the profile of most buyers who choose to buy on eBay. While fair prices can be achieved, there is a lot of pressure to sell low and to sell quickly. A seller must resist these downward pulls on their pricing. A method to potentially receive a higher payment for their car is for sellers to approach magazines for the sale. Car club magazines and generalist magazines are great for buyers of cars which are slightly more unique than average, but not quite the high-end luxury cars and collector's items that find themselves fetching top dollar. The DuPont Registry is a magazine which is well known for its high end cars, and is suitable for many exotic cars. One other method which can often fetch top dollar for highly unique cars are auctions such as the Barrett-Jackson Car Auctions. These auctions allow sellers to tap into buyers specifically looking to spend top dollar for specific cars of interest.

A seller had a low mileage, great condition, fully loaded, stock 1988 Pontiac Fiero GT. While to many this was just a "Fiero", to those who are interested in these cars, this car was the specific year, option packages, and model that buyers desperately wanted. By taking this car to EBay, the seller was able to tap into a large buying demographic, allowing him to sell the car for more than double what he paid. While EBay was a great place to sell this car, another Fiero, this time also a desirable 1988 Pontiac Fiero Formula, was not sold on eBay. It had several issues with it, and was extremely high mileage. Because it did not have the high desirability of the low mileage GT, the best place to sell it was locally and at a specialty car forum.

Cars which are not highly anticipated and desired on eBay are likely going to garner little interest. The message being sent to a potential buyer for these cars on eBay is that the seller is "just trying to unload their problem onto someone else", driving the price down. These cars are best sold on online forums and through word of mouth. EBay and Craigslist are also great places for basic cars which truly are not well desired even within specialty groups and the seller is simply trying to unload them.

The Desirability-Listing Point

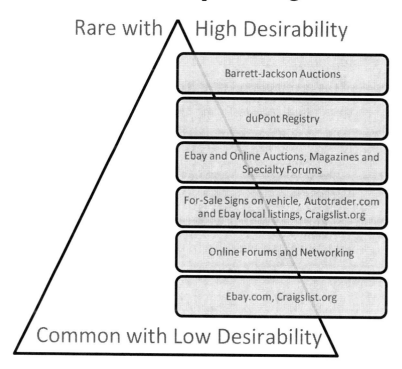

Rare with High Desirability

Barrett-Jackson Auctions

duPont Registry

Ebay and Online Auctions, Magazines and Specialty Forums

For-Sale Signs on vehicle, Autotrader.com and Ebay local listings, Craigslist.org

Online Forums and Networking

Ebay.com, Craigslist.org

Common with Low Desirability

For most cars, traditional advertising methods work effectively. These include listings on craigslist.org, Autotrader.com, eBay.com's local listings, which are different from their national auction and fixed price listings, and simple for sale signs in front of the house and around town. Ebay.com offers two listing types, one is free for up to 6 cars at a fixed price, limited to a 200 mile radius. The other is a traditional nation-wide listing which charges the seller for a completed sale. The local listing method is recommended for standard desirability cars. These cars are also often good candidates for trade-ins or direct-to-dealer sales at auction value, if timing is a concern.

Sellers may notice websites such as eBay.com and Craigslist.org are used for more desirable cars and less desirable cars, but not in between. This is because of the tendency for buyers on these websites to classify sellers into one of two extremes. Craigslist.org for example is often used by buyers to either find an "average" car, or a "cheap" car, and so those which find themselves outside of this grouping, such as a specialty car or one with some sort of unique desirability to certain buyers, listing on craigslist will leave buyers interpreting the listed car as "cheap". EBay on the other hand offers a similar concern. While occasional buyers will inspect a car on eBay prior to purchase, most buyers look at eBay as a short term, quick sale, buyer-beware, condition unknown sales method. This leaves buyers subconsciously questioning the sales motive and asking "Why is it being sold". Most will presume it is either because it is highly desirable and the car is trying to get top dollar, or the seller is trying to unload their problematic car, and therefore the buyers will lump the cars accordingly. This lowers the purchase price offers for those cars with moderate desirability. EBay Local, with its fixed price and more informal purchase process does not convey the same buying emotion which the standard eBay listings do to many buyers, which is why this sales method is listed between the others.

By choosing the correct "place" to sell a car, sellers can help ensure they are maximizing the potential value of their specific car. Sellers will find themselves in front of the type of buyers they seek to complete the sale which meets their needs and expectations.

How to Sell

Once a seller has determined where they are going to sell their car, they will then need to set their baseline price. After setting their baseline, they find how much they expect from their sale, determine their asking price, and be sure to have prepped their car for the right sales market and sales strategy.

Keep in mind that a buyer will most likely attempt to negotiate a lower rate from a seller. Sellers should be sure to set the price appropriately with the expectation that the price will be negotiated lower. At the same time, sellers can strategically determine price points to send a message about their car. A car priced higher than the baseline suggests a car in better condition than others. A car priced below the baseline suggests a car in worse condition. Improperly pricing a car does not necessarily mean it will sell faster, or for more money. Improperly pricing the car often leads to a slower sale and less money. By overpricing a car in poor condition, buyers tend to find the car for sale is not worth it, and they will either simply leave, or are more likely to generate an extremely low offer. By underpricing a car on the other hand, many buyers will not even take the time to inquire about the car as they will assume the condition based on the pricing, and may assume problems which don't even exist, leaving only those buyers where cost is more important to them than condition. Buyers who do end up looking at these under-priced cars are highly "price sensitive". Many of these buyers will be buying a car on the high end of their affordability, or will be buying a car with the expectation of spending well under list price, therefore looking at the car with the assumption that it can be negotiated lower. The best method to set the price is to establish a baseline, determine what makes the value more or less than the baseline, then set the car at a premium above this price to leave room for negotiation, typically about 8-12% higher for most cars, or about 5% higher for cars over $15,000. The list price should be compared to other cars on the market. More expensive or less expensive is perfectly acceptable, as long as the condition dictates it. Most car owners overvalue their own possessions and undervalue other's. For this reason, sellers must be careful not to overvalue their own car, no matter how easy it is for them to falsely justify their car's value.

The car should be in an appropriate condition for the type of car and the anticipated price point. From a repair perspective, this may or may not mean making necessary car repairs. A premium car, sports car, a luxury car, or exotic will typically need to be presented in near perfect condition. Unless the cost exceeds the sale price, it is typically worthwhile to make all noticeable repairs. For most cars, it is a simple "risk vs. reward" calculation to determine if the repair is worth it or not. If the car price will increase more than the repair cost, then it is worthwhile.

Extremely significant repair issues such as missing mirrors, major dents, cracked glass, and shattered bumpers are typically worth replacing. Small cracks, small dents, chips, and similar small items are not, except for the highest levels of luxury, classic, and exotic cars. Mechanical issues are more difficult to judge. Major function items, which are anything related to the driver's expected function of the car, such as the engine or transmission, driver and passenger windows, mirrors, door locks, radio, and horn should typically be repaired. Other items will depend on the type of car and its sale price. Rear window motors, a heated passenger seat, a rear speaker, or an auto dimming mirror for example may not be worthwhile replacing or repairing. Cars under $5,000 will likely not need the latter repairs, while cars over $10,000 will more likely need most of them. Those falling in between must be evaluated somewhere along the spectrum. Those around $15,000 typically should be in great shape, and those over $20,000 should mechanically be near perfect. Low-end cars, such as those under $3,000, simply need to be mechanically sound. Engine and transmission issues, starters, or battery issues are typically worth addressing. For the cheapest of cars, those under $1,000, it is not worth the investment.

From a preparation perspective, the car should align with the expectations for the car, the market, and the pricing. Some sellers frequently overprep their car, believing the cleaner and nicer the car looks, the more they will be able to sell it for. However, this may actually hurt their selling ability. Other sellers fail to take the necessary time to do the preparations they should, also hurting their selling ability. It is more important to care for the external look of the car than the interior look for most cars, as the external perspective of a car is viewed as representative of the car's mechanical condition, while the interior is representative of the seller's attitude and personality. A premium car, sports car, a luxury car, or exotic, should be shown as pristine and perfect. A full interior and exterior detailing would be appropriate. For most cars however, a detailing sends a message that the seller is demanding top dollar for the car. It may seem to many buyers that the seller is spending "excess" money on the car, or trying to "compensate" for problems with the car. Instead, it is more appropriate for sellers to clean and wax the exterior and lightly clean the interior of the car to make it look cared for, but allow it to retain its "used" look.

The price and the condition of a car are not only necessary components of a sale; they also send a message to the buyer. By maintaining the right vehicular condition, and the proper preparation for the car merged with the right pricing strategy, sellers can speed up their sale and command maximum profits from their car.

Extracting Hidden Value

When an owner has decided to sell it's usually because he or she wants something else. The excitement of "getting rid of" an old car and getting something new can lead sellers to work much less at selling and much more at buying. When selling however, a little bit of extra work and analysis can go a long way. Hidden value may exist in the car which can be used to maximize total sale price.

When discussing "buying" a car, the concept of Separable Value-Add Items, or SVAIs emerged to get an extreme deal. While SVAIs are great items to look for when buying a car because they can be turned into quick cash, they are also items to look for when selling a car. An excellent rule of thumb is that If an item isn't going to get more money than it is worth on a sale, don't include it. Instead, sell it separately. These can include things such as spare wheel sets or accessories, bed liners or brake controllers. Often these can be pulled before the sale to net a larger total payout for selling the car. More detail on SVAIs are discussed in the buying section.

By selling as many "parts" as possible separately, a seller can often see hundreds if not several thousand dollars in increased revenues. This can go a long way towards the owner's attempts to own net-neutral or net-positive. Some car owners also choose to "part-out" a car. Parting out a car means scrapping the car and selling it for parts instead of as a whole. For some cars, this can maximize value, yet it takes a significant amount of time and effort to do so, which most buyers will find not worth their time. A few SVAIs on the other hand are a great balance between simplicity and revenue maximization.

Taking Net-Positive to the Professional Level: Flipping Cars

For those looking to take Net-Positive car ownership to the next level, and utilize it as an actual profit-generation tool casually or as a full time career, the same basis for net-positive car ownership applies to flipping cars. These buyers will find that due to the hassles of buying and selling, they must work to ensure they are developing a healthy margin in their buying and selling efforts. To do so effectively, these buyers need to acquire rock bottom purchase pricing, typically requiring a certain amount of repair work to further improve value, and maximize final car sales prices by effective sales techniques.

It is essential for those choosing to do this to maintain Total Cumulative Positive Equity, or TCPE. Some individuals who choose to flip cars casually fail to properly maintain accurate records, and find that while they believe they are making money, after factoring in all perspectives of car ownership they are not. Be sure to maintain records not only of the purchase price, but of taxes, registration, insurance costs, all repair costs including transportation, wear and tear on another car to tow, haul, or just pick up repair parts, taxes, and shipping. These all quickly add up for a buyer who is not paying attention. Picking the right cars to purchase and proper planning and preparing for repairs, can create the necessary margin to not only cover the costs to maintain TCPE, but to leave enough extra money left over in the process to make it financially worthwhile.

Sellers looking to profit from "flipping cars" must be careful of local automotive dealership laws. Most states have laws preventing an individual from buying or selling more than a certain number of cars, such as 7 in any one year period. Other states require each car to be registered and have registration and tax fees based on the book value of the car, which can significantly affect the ability of an individual to flip cars. Those interested in pursuing this type of strategy should carefully research their local car dealership laws, as well as tax and registration laws, to be certain they can maintain TCPE without getting into trouble with their local governments.

Those who successfully begin to "flip cars" also need to pay attention to tax laws. These tax laws are not just the sales tax. Once the car seller makes a profit from the car, this becomes taxable income, and must be reported on income tax returns. Sellers should be sure they consult with an accountant or a tax attorney, and follow all reporting and taxing laws. These sellers will also want to ensure they factor in the taxes they must pay on their gains in evaluating their margins, and to reserve the necessary funds to make their future tax payments.

By paying attention to all costs associated with buying and selling cars, properly evaluating the markets, choosing the right cars, and buying and selling cars properly, combined with proper preparation and repair efforts, car owners can turn basic net-positive car ownership into a true profit generation tool. "Flipping cars" can generate enough profit to supplement incomes or to even maintain a reasonable income for many people.

Conclusion

In conclusion, by paying attention to the nuances of buying and selling vehicles, individuals can buy the right car for their wants and needs without breaking the bank. These buyers can properly maintain their vehicles, prep them for sale, and bring them to market at prime times. Savvy buyers and sellers can protect their financial positions during vehicle ownership, or even profit from the buying and selling process, shattering many of the commonly held notions surrounding automotive ownership.

Appendix

Notes

All research in this book was conducted by Brooks R Fiesinger. The notes below offer citations from which specific data in this book is based. All information in this book is from Primary Research completed by Brooks R Fiesinger unless otherwise acknowledged. All Car Makes and Models are Copyright their respective manufacturers.

1. http://www.consumer.ftc.gov/articles/0055-buying-used-car
2. Clough, Craig. *Why Do Mechanics Cost So Much?* 2010. Retrieved 9/11/11. http://www.lifewhile.com/cars/18803349/detail.html
3. Taylor, Alex III. Buy Here, Pay Here: Bottom-feeding for used car buyers in a recession. CNNMoney. 29, November 2010. http://money.cnn.com/2010/11/29/autos/americas_car_Mart.fortun e/index.htm
4. BMW 3-Series. MSN Autos. Accessed 8/24/2013 http://autos.msn.com/research/vip/default.aspx?ICID=HPFAC&mak e=BMW&model=3-Series&expmdl=efac#used

Case: Two is Better than One

Two cars can often be both more effective at meeting an owner's goals, and cheaper financially, than settling for a single all-in-one style vehicle selection.

For a more specific analysis, a buyer wants a Luxury Sedan to drive to and from work, for lunch meetings with clients, and to take their family on vacations. The buyer also decides they want a nice sports car to zip around town in and meet their lifelong dream of owning something truly sporty. Many people in this situation come to a logical conclusion- If they want to achieve both, they should pick up the beautiful award winning Cadillac CTS-V! While this is a logical conclusion, there may actually be a better alternative. A buyer can get an equally loaded CTS, a BMW 328i, or an Audi A4 PLUS a brand new Corvette- Even a CTS-V performance shattering Z06- all while actually saving money.

A new Cadillac CTS-V, at the time of this publishing, starts at $64,515 (before the $2,600 Gas-guzzler tax in the United States), while a non-V CTS starts at $39k, a BMW 328i starts at $33k and an Audi A4 starts at $34k. A Corvette starts at $49,600. Due to high fuel economy, the CTS, BMW, Audio, and Corvette are not subject to fuel economy taxes. While on the surface, it appears clear that the Corvette and luxury car combination is much more expensive, a deeper analysis unearths a different outcome.

After factoring in purchase prices, the next component to be factored in is the US Government Economy numbers from fueleconomy.gov. The CTS-V receives 14 MPG (combined) while the standard CTS receives 22 MPG (combined), the BMW and the Audi each gets 26 (combined). The Z06 gets 18. The base and Grand Sport (GS) Corvettes each receive 19. Going with a conservative gas price of $3.72, and assuming 15,000 annual miles over the next 5 years, Gas alone leads the CTS-V to cost over $7,000 more than the alternatives over the first 5 years of car ownership, and even more so for drivers who drive more than 15,000 miles a year, if gas prices increase, or if a buyer does significant highway driving.

The next factor to consider is resale. The BMW 328i, the Audi A4, and the Corvette all resell for a higher percentage of their initial cost than the CTS-V does based on both historical data and the overly conservative residual lease analysis data. Therefore in 5 years, a buyer is expected to lose $46k in residual value on the CTS-V, while losing as little as $27k total on a BMW and Corvette combination.

If rebates are factored in, the difference could increase by another $7500 in favor of the two-vehicle option. Currently dealerships are offering $7-9k off low level Corvettes and $6-7k off Z06s, while BMW dealerships are offering $5k off of the new BMWs. For CTS-Vs, no known dealership is offering more than $4500 off a CTS-V, increasing the difference by another $7,500. Due to the nature of the CTS-V, additional negotiations would likely not be in the CTS-V's favor either, although these were not used in analysis.

Cost savings over CTS-V			
	Car 2		
	BMW 328i	Audi A4	Cadillac CTS
Corvette z06	$8,025.08	$1,652.75	-$973.83
Corvette GS	$17,266.77	$10,894.43	$8,267.85
Corvette Base	$26,038.66	$19,666.32	$17,039.74

By combining these factors, The CTS-V will cost approximately $26k more to own than a BMW 328i + base Corvette, which is more than enough to upgrade to a much nicer luxury car, or even pick up a nice new Harley Davidson to throw into the mix. A CTS-V is even $1,600 more than an Audi and a CTS-V performance shattering Corvette Z06. These numbers are conservative estimates based on a number of assumptions which would actually increase this differential between the two. These overly conservative assumptions all act in favor of the "two-car" alternative and include:

1. Mileage is based on 15,000 miles per year and $3.72 fuel cost.
2. No car is damaged, which if one accident is assumed, would detract a higher amount from the CTS-V Resale than the car pair.
3. The cars are not modified or raced, as a researched selection of modifications are cheaper on a Corvette than a CTS-V

If any of these assumptions are factored in, based on currently available data, the numbers begin to look quite a bit different, pushing further to the "two is better than one" concept. If Gas jumps to expected levels, this raises the cost difference by up to $7,000 more.

This thought process can also offer even more tremendous gains when considering the idea of purchasing a new luxury car with a used sports car. For many people choosing to purchase multiple cars, they want a nice new car for daily driving duty, but for their sports car they are willing to accept something with a little more mileage under its belt and in non-new condition. This quickly drives the ownership costs of the "two" further below the "one" alternative, even for initial purchase prices, while meeting all of the buyer's desires.

For those who love The CTS-V, or want the performance of a CTS-V all the time, the CTS-V truly can be a logical purchase decision, and they are excellent cars. However, for those who find that the CTS-V is a cheaper way to "Settle" for what they need, those buyers may find once again that buying two instead of one actually saves them money while offering them something that is more desirable, with more performance, the same amount of luxury, and more personal satisfaction than "Settling" for the CTS-V.

This same type of evaluation also leads to a similar "Two is better than one" conclusion when evaluating other similar "all-in-ones" including luxury SUVs, Performance Trucks, Hybrids, and various other cars, making many of these vehicles a true premium luxury purchase item, and not an affordable alternative. When evaluating these factors, it becomes clear quickly that purchasing the two is superior to purchasing the one for many buyers' needs who look at the "one" as a budget alternative. For those who have a personal love and desire for a CTS-V, then it is worth the cost to make this specific purchase. Every buyer and situation is unique and different.

If you enjoyed this book, be

sure to look for other books

by Brooks R Fiesinger

To Order Bulk Quantities of:

Car$ - The Ins and Outs of

Buying and Selling

Contact the author at

BrooksFiesinger.com

CPSIA information can be obtained at www.ICGtesting.com
Printed in the USA
LVOW08s0840120616

492242LV00006B/11/P

9 781495 257025